THE HOUSE THAT

Faux Built

Transform Your Home From Shabby to Showplace
Using Paints, Plasters & Creativity

ADRIENNE VAN DOOREN

Thanks Faux Much!
Adrienne van D

YORK GRAPHIC SERVICES

York Production Services

EAST CAMBRIDGE PRESS

15876/3000

THE HOUSE THAT FAUX BUILT
Copyright © 2006 by Adrienne van Dooren

Special Edition

Photography by David Galen, Galen Photography
Additional photography provided by Omar Selinas, Suzanne Leedy and Louise Kraft

Designed by York Production Services
Brian Flaherty, Creative Director
Todd Chronister, Designer

Published by East Cambridge Press
Printed and Distributed in the U.S.A. by York Graphic Services
3650 West Market Street
York, PA 17404
www.ygsc.com

Edited by Susie Darrell-Smith

ISBN: 0-9778967-2-2

Please understand that this special draft edition was written under a 6 week deadline. Our sincere apologies for anyone we may have left
out or any mistakes. None were intentional and will be promptly corrected in the hardcover edition to be released for the general public in
the fall. Please contact us with any proposed changes at chair@fauxhouse.com.

We intend to update this book on an annual basis so that it serves as a living, growing resource. The next edition will include a "tips"
section of easy solutions to problems we learned the hard way. The 1st person to submit a tip used in the book will be credited by name.
Individuals or companies who would like to be added as sponsors, advertise their schools or products in the resources section, or take an
active role in future projects (to include a Colorado ski condo makeover and a national "Art and Ponds for Hospice" program) are welcome
to contact us as well.

Contents

Acknowledgements

I'd like to thank the Academy....no seriously, Fauxcademy, for giving me the push to get this project started. It was there that I witnessed the incredible advancements in faux and demonstrations from some of the top faux artists in the country. My gratitude goes to Mark-Victor Hansen who spoke and encouraged us all to live our dreams. This project has allowed me to do just that.

But his project isn't about me-it is about the efforts and gifts of over a hundred artists, volunteers and sponsors who came together to support hurricane victims through art.

These artists, the top in their fields, not only gave of their time and talents on very short notice, but also bore all costs of travel and expenses. Some of these artists were the instructors/mentors who helped me transition from Army to Artist (e.g .Nicola Vigini, Sean Crosby, Kelly King, Mary Kingslan-Gabilisco and Melanie Royals). Some (JoAnne Nash, Wanda Timmons, Adrian Greenfield, past classmates, and SALI members) were old friends. Others--Caroline Woldenberg, Amanda Sumerlin, Julie Miles, Brad Duerson, Tania Seabock, the Kershners, Ashley Spencer, Amy Ketteran, Deb Drager, Barth White, and others) I'd not known but asked to join based on their reputation or specialty and, like soldiers in the trenches, (yes it often felt like that), we all bonded by working toward a common goal. Indeed everyone involved in the project deserves special recognition but in the interest of our national forests each artist and room captain is featured in other portions of the book.

I would, however, like to give a special note of thanks to Ann Bayer-hospitality chair, Patti Irwin-sponsorship chair, and Celeste Stewart-operations, who made this project a near full time endeavor. Had it not been for them, the House that Faux Built would never be built.

We could not have succeeded without some incredibly dedicated volunteers. Many volunteers gave over 150hours (Carolyn Spencer, Linda O' Neill, Carl Bayer, Rebecca Hotop, Chris Jackson, Lisa Turner, Michael Gross, Ceil Glembocki , Tracie Weir, and Carol Patterson) and none complained of the mundane grunt work that is 90% of such an endeavor. Our designers, Nancy AtLee and Mau Don Nygen spent countless hours to find just the right furniture and accessories to complement the artist's work. Valerie Burchett took over as webmaster at the last minute and did a super job!

Our deepest appreciation to all our sponsors who gave selflessly in support of this project, with a special note of thanks to Modello Designs™ - decorative masking pattern, Artimatrix and Faux Effects® International for being the first to support the project when it was only a concept with absolutely no guarantee of success.

My friends Suzanne Leedy and Susie Darrell-Smith not only served as board members but also kept me fed and sane during the process. Thanks to Cynthia Haig for introducing me to the business and to my good friends Ernie Dominguez and family, Mike and Peg San Roman, Barb and Vic Tise, Roger Dimsdale, John and Maurine Dubia, Kim Wadford, and Barb Trent for providing critical emotional support.

I also owe a very deep note of gratitude to those who helped me to develop the leadership skills and courage to take on such a project: Dean Larry Wilson and Montreat College, SGM Jimmie Spencer, SGM Don Airhart, MSG Ray Wilson, LTC Darrell Best, Col William L. Hart, Col John Spears, LTG Tom Plewes, LTG John Pickler, Richard and Vicki Scherberger, Col Crissy Gayagas, Gen and Mrs Denny Reimer and MG Wallace.

Mentors often include those in the media. Many books and personalities have made a major impact on the way I view the world: Wayne Dyer (You'll See it When You Believe It, No Limit Person, etc), Joe Dominguez and Vicky Robin –(Your Money or Your Life) Oprah Winfrey (Inspirational Shows and her life and spirit in general), HGTV (home makeover ideas) Dr Phil-(just do it/no nonsense message), Martha Stewart and Andrea Stoddard (how to make the everyday beautiful.) Anthony Robins (Books on tape series), Robert Redford (Building Sundance / ongoing environmental work) our library system for a world of free art education, and to my publisher…especially Brian Flaherty, Matt Meyers, Marilyn Ross and Todd Chronister.

Last but not least, a special note of thanks to my family: My mother, going through a difficult transition herself, had to put up with 9 months of my absence due to total involvement in this project. Thanks for understanding Mom. My brothers, Bill and Leo helped with supportive phone calls; sadly Leo tragically died in a skiing accident just as the house was nearing completion.

My brother Robert and his partner Elly, have always inspired me with their incredible creativity and ability to make a house a home-even when that "house" is a sailboat. The Passmanns, my adoptive family, have shared 25 magical German Christmases in their ultimate loving, warm and cozy home. My honorary brother, Gary, is not only supportive but is like human Prozac--he can't help but lift one's spirits.

While no longer alive, my father instilled in me the ability to take risks, not to fear the unknown and just jump right in.

Last, John David, my twin brother and Priest of The Church of the Atonement certainly bent over backwards to help. Having often been on the receiving end of my overzealous creativity, he was somewhat dubious, yet allowed us to add his church and rectory to the project in order to accommodate a greater number of talented artists. In the end, of course, he was thrilled…and yes, I think a bit surprised.

To say that The House that Faux Built has been a salutary experience for me would be a grave understatement on many levels. Adrienne's initial conception for this project was during one of our many "happy hour wine and canapé" evenings, needless to say it seemed like the most perfect idea she had ever had!

Little did we all realize that this was one of the things that she would that she would remember the next day, simply because she had been determined to do it in the first place and had used our gathering as the forum to float the idea.

When I first saw the house that she had chosen, my heart sank, while it was in a very good neighborhood it was expensive, particularly unattractive and sorely lacking (in my opinion) the potential required to turn it into the masterpiece Adrienne had envisioned. Needless to say I voiced my opinions strongly to the other Board members and into several glasses of wine over the following weeks!

I refused to visit the house to view the work in progress, (as it turns out denying myself the opportunity of meeting amazing artists who had traveled nationally and internationally) insisting to Adrienne that I was "saving myself for the finished product!"

That day finally came. As we parked at the house I was immediately overwhelmed by the new look of the exterior including, but not limited to, the new landscaping, path leading to the front door, new look of the shed, stairs leading to the back entrance, the fountain and essentially the wonderful ambiance and overall peaceful feeling that this engendered. All this before I had even entered the house!

Suffice it to say that I have never experienced the overwhelming emotion that literally left me speechless as I toured the house. Each and every room, hallway, closet and bathroom is truly an exercise in artistic triumph. Each time I thought that I had seen the most magnificent work possible and I moved on to the next area I was, yet again, proven wrong!

This house is a living, breathing, breathtaking example of an inspired and humanitarian idea by Adrienne van Dooren, brought to life by the top artists nationally and internationally, who so generously gave of their amazing talents and time.

Susie Darrell-Smith

I'm often asked how this project came about. It started as a thought; an idea that expanded into action as many artists shared the same vision. In the end the project exceeded all expectations, becoming the decorative artisan's version of "We are the World."   Over a hundred top artists worked together in "concert" to fund a House to be built by Habitat for Humanity-New Orleans for Katrina victims. For that reason the project has been dubbed "*The House that Faux Built* . An international birdhouse painting contest was added to aid the animals made homeless by the hurricanes and to insure that any artist who wanted to participate in this project could do so.

 Once funded, many of the artists and volunteers will also go to New Orleans to work on the Habitat house.   A portion of proceeds from the sale of this book will go to Habitat-New Orleans to continue this work, with the remainder reimbursing past costs of keeping the house unoccupied and helping to fund future projects. Many people ask what will happen to the house. We are renting it out furnished, to allow limited access for the media, to preserve the art and to test under real conditions the long-term durability of the finishes.

It is also our hope that this book will increase public awareness of the incredible advances in faux and decorative painting since the sponging fad of the 90's and serve as a catalyst for ideas and further advancements in decorative painting.

Adrienne van Dooren

Artist Barth White custom mixed a palette of golden earth tones to complement the warm wood tones in the floor. He and his team troweled the walls with several layers of natural limed based marmorino by Rivedil.™ The plaster imparts an aged Italian feel to the room and provides a warmth impossible to mimic with paint.

Living Room

This cozy living room invites you to sit and relax and enjoy the warmth of the fire.

The living room should be the heart of the home, but the 1940s red brick fireplace and ceramic tile hearth made the room appear dated and unattractive. The fireplace seemed too tall for the room and the small sconces were lost on the wall.

Before

The red brick of the fireplace was first primed, then painted and glazed with soft metallic paint by Ralph Lauren. Quartzstone™ was troweled over the dated red ceramic hearth to give it the look of the look of a solid stone slab.

A custom cut stencil was added to the walls using lime paint to complement the design on the floor.

Stewart Kershner of Beaux-Artes created an over-mantel out of simple MDF board which he decoratively routed then added a glued-on resin trim piece. Once painted, the over-mantle established the fireplace as an attractive focal point and helped to ground the room.

A comparison of this before shot of the living room wall opposite the fireplace illustrates the power of paints and plasters to completely transform a space from cold and boring to warm and wow! The artist's color choices tie together the living room, hall and kitchen for a far more harmonious look. This is important given the openness of this floor plan.

Before

To further soften the room and make the ceiling appear higher, he then matched a paint /glaze mixture to the wall color and applied it to the white ceiling using a sprayer and his signature Faux Tool.

In order to distress and age and fireplace surround and trim, Barth first painted them a dark brown, then applied crackle medium and glazes. He later used sandpaper to remove paint in raised areas for a distressed look. His trim color is only slightly darker than the walls, thus unifying the room. The result? Stunning!

Guest artist and author, Melanie Royals of San Diego taught a group of volunteers how to apply a 6' x 8' Modello Decorative Masking Pattern™ (a one-time-use, adhesive vinyl stencil) to create an incredible "carpet" of faux inlaid wood. They used water-based gel Stain and Seal™ to stencil the various colors through the elaborate pattern. Modello Designs™ have revolutionized the faux world by allowing intricate patterns to be produced less expensively and on a large scale. For this floor project the masking pattern was also useful in insuring against the "bleed under" that can be problematic when using mylar stencils.

4

Ann and Carl preparing floor

Before >

The original floors were covered with beige carpet. While worn, they were in better shape than the wood parquet floor beneath. Over the years of multiple rentals, the floor had suffered from water damage, grime, pet stains and dripped paint. A professional floor finishing company deemed it beyond repair and recommended we replace it. Unwilling to rip out if there was any hope, Ann Bayer and husband Carl decided to tackle it. By sanding and then applying wood bleach, they were able to lessen the contrast between the dark pet stains and lighter woods. Hand applied wood putty filled in cracks. This was followed by more sanding, a sealer and light stain. Was it worth it? While a huge amount of work, they were rewarded with a beautifully unique patterned floor.

This yard sale table with a parquet pattern seemed a perfect fit for the room. Ann Bayer refinished it and stained it to complement the floor.

Artists

Barth White-walls, ceiling and trim
Melanie Royals- faux inlay floor and Modello™ class
Anne Bayer-Room Captain, hearth & table
Stuart Kershner- grates and moldings
Carl Bayer: floor preparation
Debbie Thompson: picture framing
Team Members: Sandi Anderson, Melissa Clements, Tania Seabock, Rosalie Myers, Rebecca Hotop, Sandra Davis, Mitch Eanes, and Pauline Siple.

Sponsors

Amaze-a-Glaze™
Arlington Paint and Decorating Center-painting supplies
Beaux-Artes- decorative vents, moldings and fireplace topper
Color Wheel-Benjamin Moore, Adicolor, and Lime Seal
Decorator's Supply Warehouse-composite molding piece

Designers- Nancy AtLee and Mau Don Nuyen
Dominion Floors- final sealing of floors
Faux and Fleur Designs- hand painted table
Faux Effects® International- Stain & Seal™, FX Thinner™ & sealers
Hanging Treasures-frames
Mann Brothers Casein
Mixol™ Tints
Modello Designs™ – decorative masking pattern
Modern Masters- Satin Varnish
Ralph Lauren- metallic paints
Store House Furniture- chairs, window coverings and accessories
The Faux School- Rivedil™ wall and ceiling products
The Faux Tool™
Voss Creative- custom stencil
Westover Florist- fresh flowers

6

This elegant dining room was once a seldom used brick porch. The panoramic windows coupled with the natural flow from indoor living areas to the casual dining patio made this room ideally suited for a buffet station for large parties or a romantic dinner for two.

This incredible transformation was again accomplished with paint and plaster. The grey cement floor was painted in an inlay wood and marble pattern, windows and moldings wood grained, brick walls plastered in an elegant sage Lusterstone™ and the dated bead-board ceiling covered by a painted canvas.

Before

Tania designed the mural and drew it out on heavy canvas cut to fit the ceiling. She painted it in pigments she mixed with acrylic medium, creative a beautiful micro-mosaic pattern. Mounting the heavy canvas to the ceiling took several volunteers and extra heavy duty adhesive.

The bead-board insets were covered with very thin sheets polystyrene plastic, then fauxed in a walnut burl. Composite molding was painted, gilded and glued to the top and bottom of each panel to mimic expensive carved wood.

This window-sill was hand molded using Scagliola (Sca-li-o-la), an old world European technique from the 1500s invented to imitate Pietra Dura (inlay stones.) Tania is one of a very few restorative artists in the US skilled in this technique. She used a negative mold created to fit the window sill and a mixtur of plaster, rabbit skin glue, pigment, lime and a lot of sanding. Once smooth, she applied a final coat c linseed oil for a beautiful satin sheen.

The brick walls were troweled with a mixture of Dryloc™ moisture sealing paint and drywall powder, followed by several layers of Lusterstone in a mix of olive and gold. The walls now have a beautiful shimmer and perfectly complement the silk curtains.

Beaux-Artes hinge-straps were glued adjacent to the existing hinges for an added decorative element.

A Beaux-Artes door escutcheon was glued right around the existing knob for an easy and elegant custom look. Modello™ stencils and window frosting craft paints were used to create the "etched" glass designs.

This faux inlay marble and wood floor was painted over the existing concrete and sealed well to withstand foot traffic.

Room Captain, Tania Seabock beginning the wood grain.

A New Orleans Matchbook painted by Ashley Spencer reminds visitors of the purpose of the project. The matchbook is so realistic, even the other artists have tried to pick it up.

Room Captain Tania Seabock designed the floor to complement the lines of the door's glass panels and provide a contrast to the curves of her ceiling mural. She masked out the pattern with 1/8th inch tape and used the classic European method of creating realistic woods and marbles with beer and pigment and artist's oil paints. Tania first painted the marble. The larger squares were done in a faux grey breche and the accent pieces in yellow sienna. She then retaped the floor and completed the wood-graining process. The floor took a total of five days to complete.

Artists

Tania Seabock –Room Captain, wood graining, floor, ceiling, windowsill, gilding, icon
Carol Patterson –Room Lieutenant, walls
Adrienne van Dooren –general design &color choices
Rebecca Hotop–frosted Modello™ window patterns
Ashley Spencer– trompe' l oeil matchbook
Ceil Glemblocki –window treatments and flower arrangements
Team Members: Ian Seabock, Hector Lopez, Lisa Turner, John Lernard Stuart Kershne, Caroline Spencer, Steve Brown

Sponsors

Andreae Stencils–trowels
Arlington Paint and Decorating Center– paints, varnishes, and supplies
Art Stuf– moldmaking materials, plasters, waxes, fiberglass, pigments, and adhesives
Beaux-Arts–Composite moldings, door hinge straps and door knob
Calico Corners–window treatment hardware and decorative tassels
Color Wheel – Benjamin Moore Paints and Versiplast™
Discount Fabrics USA - drapery fabric
Faux Effects®International–Lusterstone™ and supplies
Faux Fingers–small trowels
Golden paints –acrylic ground, absorbent ground and acrylic modifier for plaster
Plaza Arts– oil paints, brushes and other necessary items
Royal Design Studio–panel design stencils for side windows
Sinopia–raw powdered pigments, gold leaf, and artist's brushes
Steve Brown Construction–trim
Modello Designs™ - decorative masking pattern for small window panes
Thompson Creek –bay and picture windows and copper roof on the exterior of the house to replace the 1940s, non-energy efficient windows.

Caroline carefully selected colors to create this old world warmth. The walls and ceiling were glazed in yellow ochre tones, the cabinetry in Italian sienna and the trim in teal. The complementary teal trim brings excitement to this small kitchen, giving every detail more emphasis and visual impact.

A major goal of the Fauxhouse was to show that it is possible to make use of what you have without expensive remodeling. In that spirit, we salvaged the cabinets, refrigerator, dishwasher and disposal. However, the 1940s kitchen was so small that you could not open the refrigerator door without moving to the side. Therefore, we decided to tear out the non-load bearing wall between the kitchen and dining room to create an eat-in kitchen where the family could gather.

Before

Caroline Woldenberg based her concept for the kitchen on her experiences visiting and working in European kitchens. These spaces were often small but served as the heart of the home. She was particularly impressed by the centuries old walls which bore witness to the passage of time; yet, despite the well worn surfaces, were clean and comfortable, encouraging one to linger over a meal.

By purchasing 6 additional builder's grade Lowes cabinets and rearranging those we had, costs were kept to a minimum. Caroline Woldenberg of The Finishing Source, Inc. chose to top the cabinets with inexpensive wood molding and stagger the height for an expensive custom look. She also brought forward the cabinets on the left and right of the stove and above the refrigerator to make the appliances look built –in. Caroline and her team spent many hours preparing the cabinets and box seat to make them perfectly smooth before painting. They first deglossed the cabinets, then applied Master Finishing Medium™ to fill the wood grain and sanded using fine grit sandpaper. They painted the cabinets with a 4-stage sprayer and Setcoat™, a self leveling, long lasting basecoat and primer in one. An antiquing glaze coupled with subtle striae and splatter give the cabinets a rich, timeless finish.

Kitchen

Remodeling doesn't have to
mean ripping out...

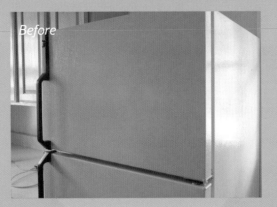

Before

The 1970s style textured refrigerator was
customized by attaching routed MDF board
and new handles. Amanda Sammelin used
a magnetic paint additive to ensure artwork
could still be hung on the door. Both the
refrigerator and dishwasher was carefully
primed and painted to match the cabinets.
While the stove was operational and could
have been painted with specialty heat
resistant paint, it was large and dated, so
They opted for a new stainless steel model
to serve as a focal point in the center of the
room

Wanda Timmons of Designer Finishes, Il, sponged
various colors of Venetian Gem™ knocked down
with a trowel to the kitchen countertop, creating a
very realistic faux granite. These countertops were
made of inexpensive ply-wood and trim, however,
this finish can also be used over properly prepared
Formica. Wanda applied a brown glaze to tie the
colors together and several coats of sealer to
protect the finish.   A new inexpensive but stylish
faucet completes the update.

Dan Mahlmann and Gary Arvanitopulos finished the buffet-style counter to resemble stone using a troweled on cement overlay. The "inlay" strip was taped off and tinted in sienna tones to complement the cabinetry.

The cabinets were actually the upper cabinets above the dishwasher in the before photo. The 12" depth was perfect for the narrow passage area. Small wooden shelves were added on either end for a more built-in look. Painted in Umbria, Italy by artist Nicola Virgini, this beautiful grotesca canvas hangs on the wall above the buffet.

15

Caroline Woldenberg used tape and marmarino plaster to create a back-splash of very convincing faux tile. She added Venetian plaster diamonds to match the countertop and tie the two spaces together.

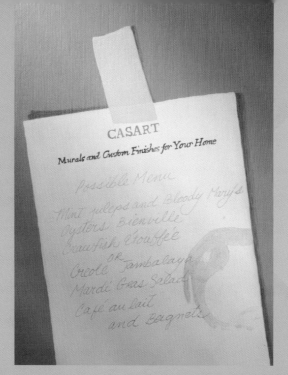

A note and masking tape were painted on kitchen door complete with a "coffee stain" and Cajun menu. Artist Ashley Spencer is a New Orleans native and has donated hundreds of hours to help those in her hometown after the tragic flooding.

Artists

Caroline Woldenberg –Room Captain and Designer
Amanda Summerlin-Co-Room Captain
Wanda Timmons- Venecian Plaster Countertop
Dan Mahlmann- cement overlay countertop
Gary Arvanitopulos- cement overlay countertop
Nicolla Vigini- Grotesca Panel
Ashley Spencer- trompe l'oeil note
Patti Irwin-kitchen table
Team Members: Jenny Vanier-Walter, Maureen M. Watkins, Carolyn Spencer, Carol Patterson, Debbie Dennis, Julie Miles, Kimberly Bohn, Carl Bayer, Russell Sellineer, Reginald Flemming, Lewis Lewis, Sheri Anderson, Sandra Davis, Susan Huber, Pauline Sipple, Ceil Glemblocki, Stuart Kershner, Robin Bear, and Shireen Balkissoon

Patti Irwin, MD, painted a $10 yard sale table to match both the curtain design and the Tuscan theme of the room. Shireen Balkissoon painted a side table in similar colors and style.

Caroline and her team used a vertical wall plastering technique to emphasize height and make the ceiling seem higher. Matching the ceiling color to the walls also has this effect since you see no harsh line between the ochre wall and a white ceiling. You won't find a white ceiling in the faux house. She aged the newly plastered wall using RS Series™ glaze and activator by Faux Effects® International. A concrete overlay" flagstone" floor in very similar tones further unifies the room.

Sponsors

Arlington Paint & Decorating Center –supplies
Beaux-Artes-vent cover and refrigerator panels
Bray and Scarff, Lee Hwy-stainless steel stove
Calico Corners- window coverings & bench seat cushions
DC Concrete Technologies-floor materials
Faux Effects® International-paints, plasters, materials and sealers
Hanging Treatures-frames
Globe Kitchen and Bath-construction support and permits
Krylon Paints-magnetic and chalkboard paints
Decorative Concrete of Maryland, Inc-countertop materials
Micheal gross -trashcan
The Finishing Source, Inc, Atlanta

A stark and uninviting white stairwell became one of the most fascinating and dynamic parts of the house, thanks to Artist, Amy Ketteran.

The top of the stairs now lead down to a lovely trompe l' oeil mural portraying the entance to a home library, rather than a blank white wall. The mural visually adds interest and expands the space.

Before

Before

The grey carpet was removed to reveal the oak beneath. Artist Amy Ketteran of MD then dressed up the wooden steps and landing with with a cartouche and harlequin diamonds. She first painted the cartouche mural on TFR in her Maryland studio. She choose sepia tone on tone to complement the red oak. Amy later cut the mural into 14 strips and pasted each to the face of a step using a clay adhesive. Two coats of sealer help protect against scuff marks. The diamond pattern was created with tape, painted with Behr porch paint and later sanded to age and distress it so that it would feel original to the home.

This Westie fooled visitors who often petted him before realizing they have been tromphed! Reactions were strong as folks either loved it or were disturbed by it. Once Adrienne's dog, he was preserved after a tragic accident by KeepMyPet.com. They use a special freeze drying method which, unlike taxidermy, preserves the "personality" of the pet.

At the top of the stairs a once boring landing is now hosts a reading nook. The project was a family affair; Amy's husband built a cozy reading nook in the opening between two hall closets. The seat lifts up for storage and the decorative vent allows for air circulation.

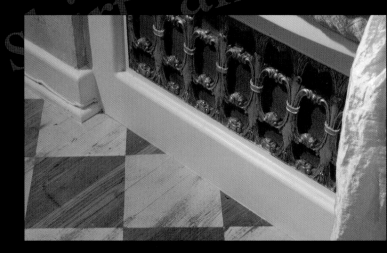

Amy had regular mirrors cut to size and chemically removed the black paint from the back. Using an antique mirror patina solution kit she distressed and aged the mirror. Then using a modello stencil, she removed the silver backing from the exposed areas of the stencil replacing it with gold paint. Once dry, she painted the entire back of the mirror with a partial coat of brown spray paint followed by 2 coats of black spray paint and a shellac sealer. The mirrors were attached in the door panels using mastic.

moment to lose. You must st

cations at once! Wash your fac

your hair, scrub your hands,

your teeth. Blow your nose c

hoes, iron your shirt, and

Amy painted her German shepherd into the panel at the base of the steps. A real rope toy and bowl placed at the foot of the mural adds both depth and realism.

Panel for Steps   Painted niche and flower vase.

Artists
Amy Ketteran-Room Captain/Murals
Andra Held-Faux Finisher
Team Members: Sandra Davis, Joan Hagan, Mark, Ketteran, Pauline Siple, Caroline Spencer, Francesca Springolo, Karen Steele, Chris Woodruff

Sponsors
Behr-porch paint
Dominion floors-final floor finish
Faux Effects® International-Aquastone and wall finish/ sealing products
Keepmypet.com-preserved pet
Plaza Arts: Delta acrylics
Plaid metallic paints Modello Designs™ - decorative masking pattern
The Mad Stencilist-"Say What" Stencils
Tim Poe-Mirror Aging Chemicals

The use of aquastone and "Say What" Vinyl Adhesive Word Stencils sped the task up considerably. The quotes appear faded and aged, yet have a light metallic glow.

Crossroads to Culture

The "Crossroads to Culture" room combines Moroccan, Moorish, and Indian Designs. The room beckons you to sit and immerse yourself in the magic of the East

Landscape murals are an excellent way to visually enhance a room. This original mural-on-canvas was painted at The International Salon of Decorative Painters by four respected and accomplished artisans: Pascal Amblard, Sean Crosby, Pierre Finkelstein and Nicola Vigini. This original composition depicts a seated figure in a traditional sari overlooking a tranquil landscape in Northern India. The woman depicted in the panel is the wife of muralist Sean Crosby.

Before

Crossroads to Culture

The oversized ceiling-fan made this tiny master bedroom appear even smaller. White walls and taupe carpet were neutral but uninspiring. Many homeowners believe that white rooms and white ceilings make rooms look larger. In truth, bold colors often give a room presence making it seem more spacious. Such was the case in this master bedroom. Plastered in a bold red, the room appears larger and more welcoming. The hardwood floors, teak furniture, and earth-toned ceiling keep the red from being too overwhelming.

Photo by Louise Craft

Designer Mau Don Nuyen applies gold highlights to brighten this pretty but dully colored mirror to complement the gold tones of the wall. She then positioned the mirror to reflect the landscape mural, thus adding light and visual depth to the room.

Artist Ron Layman chose a beautiful Rivedil™ Venetian plaster for the walls. For additional interest, created two accent walls by using a crackle medium under the final layer of plaster. Once the cracks formed he then applied a gold wax, thus defining the cracks and subtly softening the wall color.

An embedded Modello™ design in Venetian plaster creates a focal point on one wall.

The ceiling, or "5th wall" is too often ignored by homeowners. A white ceiling certainly would not complement the red plastered walls. Ron fauxed the ceiling with a wax in subtle earth tones. The oversized fan was removed and replaced with a small light proportionate with the small space. The red glass casts a lustrous red light pattern across the ceiling, which, when it deepens at night, has a truly magical feel and serves to unite the red walls and earth toned ceiling.

Ron Layman used a Modello™ adhesive stencil and a henna colored stain to enhance the hardwood floors. He then mirrored the medallion design on the ceiling.

Two-toned finish was used in the closet. Ron Layman used Silk Paint in Ruggine Rossa for the upper portion and a more textured product, Terra I'Talia in Mattone for the lower. Designer Nancy AtLee dressed the closet with authentic Moroccan garb and added beaded trim for interest. She carried the same beading around the bedroom's ceiling rather than traditional molding to enhance the overall multi-cultural theme

John and Mike mixing

Mike Bedster graining door.

The wood graining is accomplished in several layers to achieve depth. The panel above shows the straw yellow basecoat and the first layer of graining.

The trim and doors were painted white and would not have complemented the new red walls-In fact no paint color would have given the warmth of wood. Adding all new molding and doors was not an option. Artists Mike Bedster of England and John Leonard of Arlington used old fashioned European beer based wood graining techniques and oil paints to simulate a rare wood. The result is luminous and totally convincing.

Artists

Ronald Layman-Primary Artist/Room Captain
Tracy Weir- Co-Room Lieutenant
Lisa Turner- Co Room Lieutenant
John Leonard-wood graining prep and support
Mike Bedster (England)-wood graining
Rebecca Hotop –donated table
Crosby - Combined Mural Panel
Pascal Amblard- Combined Mural Panel Mural
Nicola Vigini- Combined Mural Panel
Pierre Finkelstein-Combined Mural Panel
Deborah Thompson-Stretching canvas mural
Mau Don Nuyen-Designer
Nancy AtLey-Designer

Sponsors

Arlington Paints and Decorating
Crosby–Amblard Studios
Hanging treasures
The Faux SchoolTerra I'Talia, Décor Fondo, Rivedil™, Modern Masters
The Store House
Modello Designs™- decorative masking patterns for floor, ceiling and wall

29

The master bath was small and dated. Built in the 1940s, it had never been remodeled. The white tile had yellowed over the years and the grey and white floor tile had a huge crack running across the entire floor.

While doing research for the theme, the artists discovered a multitude of embellishment options. Moroccan architectural elements are filled with pattern within patterns and a variety of designs which Donna and Deb were able to incorporate by using various stencil motifs. They chose neutral earth-tones resembling tumbled marble throughout the middle of the space. There was no need to rip out existing tile. Specialty etching creams, primers, stone-like plasters and sealers enable faux finishers to create a lasting watertight finish. A faux stone sink and toilet seat replaced the old fixtures. The crowning touch to the room is the larg CoralLight™ faux stone trim. Incredibly realistic, yet weighing only five pounds, thi interior/ exterior molded "stone" was easily cut and glued to the tub front.

Deb and Donna had originally planned to put the palm pattern on the walls. However, upon their first observations of the actual space, they felt the ceiling had so much presence that they switched their idea. They placed the color and the main pattern on this arched architecture as it provides the main focal point of the small room. Placing random large patterns above eye-level can create drama and make the ceiling appear to have more height. This switch balanced and connected visually to the faux slate floor, with the olive, bronze, and sage LusterStone™ which an chors the room. The illusion of a small window was included to give the room mor visual depth. Through the window, far-away clouds shimmer with subtle metallic effects, bouncing light and reminding one of a sunrise.

Before

Artists Deb Drager and Donna Phelps transformed the 1940s white on white bathroom into a small Moroccan retreat with carved stone elements.

The "D" Team Donna Phelps, Donna Smith and Deb Drager.

Faux stone sink with faux bronzed pipes was made by Laura Nalley and adds color and texture to the room.

Artists

Deb Drager – Co-Room Captain
Donna Phelps – Co-Room Captain
Laura Nalley– mosaic mirror
Team members: Steve Brown, Celeste Stewart, and Carolyn Spencer

Sponsors

Art-i-Matrix Academy of Architectural Finishes
Beaux Artes – decorative grate
Coral-Lite (distributed by Art-i-Matrix)
Faux Effects® International
Noland Plumbing
Lowes-light
Royal Design Studio-stencils
The Studio Collection by Donna Phelps, Inc.
Sarasota School of Decorative Artes

The main Moroccan Medallion motif was accomplished with a heavy 14mil raised plaster stencil from the Victoria Larsen Exclusive Professional Collection. The Sarasota School of Decorative Arts, Inc. distributes the stencil line, available only to Faux Finishing Schools and industry professionals" to "The Sarasota School of Decorative Arts, Inc. distributes the stencil line exclusively to Faux Finishing Schools and Industry Professionals. Donna selected this pattern and creatively portrayed it as both carved stone and as a faux silver platter hung from the wall.

This room presented four major challenges: it's small dimensions, a curved ceiling on only one wall, two very different window sizes, and an awkward placement of doors leading into the hallway and closet.

The carpet was discarded and beautiful hardwood floors revealed beneath. While some damaged wood had to be replaced, the new wood matches beautifully. Joanne chose a warm golden glaze for the walls and ceiling using a chamois cloth for application. She selected pale blue as her accent color to complement the gold and draw the eye around the room.

A hand painted ceiling border serves to define the otherwise awkwardly curved ceiling as a distinctive and lovely architectural feature.

32

Romantic Bedroom

Artist Joanne Nash wanted this room to capture the feel of a romantic European era. Her choice of French styled fabrics, Italian scrollwork and Dutch tile all work together to create a wonderful vintage feel. The light color values selected for the walls and ceiling make the room feel airy and bright but at the same time, relaxing.

Design elements from the border were then carried throughout the room on door panels, trompe l'oeil moldings, fireplace trim and painted rug.

Joanne found the perfect fabric for the bed throw and accent pillow; however, the colors were too strong and vibrant for the vintage feel. To solve this problem, she first soaked the fabric in a mild bleach solution, then in a solution of tea and water and later dried it in the sun.

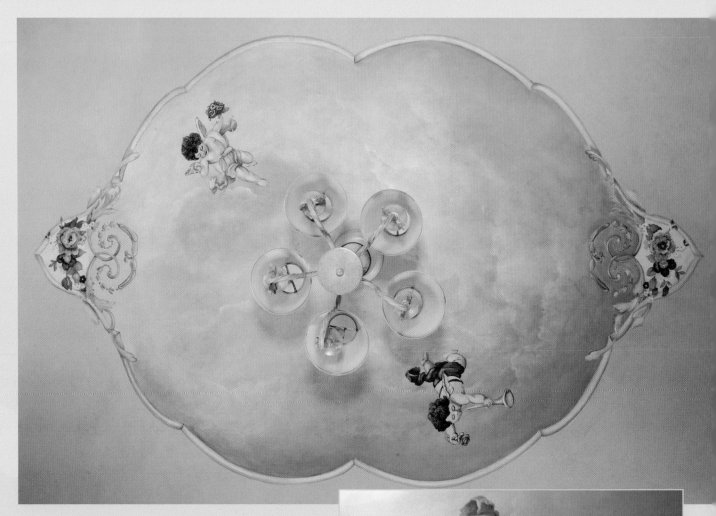

The ceiling mural was designed and painted on canvas in the studio and installed on site. An inexpensive chandelier was painted and the small shades decorated with beaded trim to complement the mural.

Joanne painted and distressed the doors of a salvaged armoire to match the fabric. As a last detail, she located a ceramic figurine in a thrift store and painted the dress to match the woman in the fabric.

Romantic Closet

Ashley Spencer took a boring white Closet and added fun Trompe L' Oeil elements to include a painted silk robe, shoes, purses, love letters, a pen and an inkwell. Ashley used stencils for the shoes and purses but hand painted the robe and love letters using the real items for reference.

The result is so realistic that many visitors ignore them believing they are real and staged as props. Ashley did add real props-a real purse, tie and necklaces and padded hangers which add a great deal of depth and aid in the illusion.

Before

This room presented four major challenges: it's small scale, a curved ceiling on only one wall, two very different window sizes, and an awkward placement of doors leading into the hallway and closet.

The carpet was discarded and beautiful hardwood floors revealed beneath. While some damaged wood had to be replaced, the new wood matches beautifully. Joanne chose a warm golden glaze for the walls and ceiling using a chamois cloth for application. She selected pale blue as her accent color to complement the gold and draw the eye around the room. Artist Rebecca Hotop used a grotesca style stencil similar to Joanne's designs to decorate the closet door. She then added hand embellishments to add depth and beauty.

Rebecca also stenciled a hat hanging on a nail on the inside of the door and a cute mouse going in his hole near the fireplace. Again, hand embellishments and shading make the hat and mouse more realistic.

Faux molding

This hand painted ceiling border serves to define the otherwise awkwardly curved ceiling as a distinctive and lovely architectural feature.

Fireplace built by Dennis Nash

Dutch tile panel by Adrian Greenfield

Left to Right: Joanne Nash, Adrian Greenfield Belinda Yoder and Rebecca Hotop

What could be more romantic than a fireplace? Since a real fireplace wasn't an option, Dennis Nash built mantle and hearth designed to be easily installed and removed without major damage to the wall. The replace's design allows 3x3' canvas inserts to changed out to fit any mood or season.

heated wax adhesive makes it easy to place, adjust ad remove with no mess. Guest artist Adrian Greenfield f England painted the primary panel tile and brick with such realism that many who visit are fooled by it. o add a touch of whimsy he added a painted Westie sitting inside, apparently ready to play with a ball.

Burning candles panel by Kate Nagel

Classical panel by Francesca Springolo

Artists

Joanne Nash - Room Captain
Adrian Greenfield - Guest Artist, England
Rebecca Hotop - Room Lieutenant, door, mouse
    and floor cloth
Kate Nagle - Fireplace Insert - candles
Francesca Springolo - Fireplace Insert - classical
Belinda Yoder - window treatments and bedding
Dennis Nash - Carpentry fireplace and bed
Ashley Spencer - Romantic Closet

Sponsors

Andreae Stencils - stencils
Beaux-Artes - decorative grate
Cheri Perry - displayed bird house for Noah's
    Wish auction
Decorator's Supply - add-on molding for bed and
    end table
Faux Effects® International - paints, glazes and
    sealers
Mad Stencilist - wax adhesive
PRO FAUX - JewelStone ceiling finish in closet,
    gold wax
Sabina and Sullivan/ Discount Fabrics USA -
    accent pillow and bed throw fabric
Roc-lon, Inc. - canvas for ceiling and floor cloth
Decorative grate - Beaux-Artes
Floor repair - Hatcher's Floors

Melanie Kershner Artist and Designer for Beaux-Artes Division of Heavenly Home Designs created a heavenly fantasy for the fauxhouse nursery. he room was transformed from a storage closet with badly stained floors into a magical land of fairies high above the clouds. To achieve this ethereal feeling, Melanie created soft billowy pastel clouds on the ceiling and walls using a HVLP sprayer. She also painted cloud tops on a wall to wall floor cloth to cover the stained wooden floor. A phosphorescent fairy looks down through an "opening" in the clouds to see the Mediterranean coastline twinkling with glowing points of light.

Wooden window and door cornices were finished in a pale blue Venetian plaster, then decorated using Pearl palette deco on Modello™ adhesive stencils, with faux gemstones o look like crowns.

The nursery could not officially be considered a third bedroom because it did not have a closet. We solved the closet issue by bumping a hole into the hall closet and adding a small custom door.

Before

39

Melanie stenciled the mural in acrylics, then hand embellished and shaded for depth. Once dry, she went over the areas she wanted to glow with phosphorescent pigment mixed with glaze and hand-painted tiny stars on the ceiling and walls. The pigments are invisible until the room is darkened. The phosphorescent mineral pigments have a richer look than typical glow in the dark paint since they are applied over whatever color palette you choose. The glow will last up to 12 hours.

Adding to the mystical feel of the room is the Luminex curtain with interwoven fiber optics. Operating on either AC or batter power it twinkles softly without over-lighting the room.

The door was embellished to look like a Pearly Gate using a Modello™ design with Pearl Palette Deco. The decorative knob was made from a drapery tieback finial.

elanie painted the basinet and rocking chair using pearlescent ints and adding faux jewels, making the rocking chair seem most like a throne. The room's evening glow acts as a night ght for a mother to nurse in this chair, comforting the baby and joying the dark; no need to turn the lights on.

Artist Melanie Kershner

Whimsical fairies are blowing crystal "fairy dust" or throwing colorful rhinestone stars into the air. Pegasus has wings of sparkle paste to catch the baby's attention as it changes

Day

Night

Artists

Melanie Kershner - Room Captain
Linda O'Neill - Room Lieutenant
Stuart Kershner - Moldings/door/grate/cornices
Wanda Swierczynski - Sewing
Ceil Glembloci - Blackout curtain

Sponsors

Faux Effects® International: Basecoat, Pallet Decco, Sealers
Modello ™ - Adhesive stencil designs on cornice and door designs
Heavenly Home Designs - phosphorescent pigments
Color Wheel - Benjamin Moore paints
Roc-lon - floor cloth and window shades
Stencil Kingdom - architectural stencils and fairies
Andreae Stencils - garden fairy stencil sets
Buckingham Stencils - cornice angels
Beaux-Arts - Moldings, vents, door and cornices

41

Before

Rather than fight the low ceiling, Adrienne decided to embrace it by applying a pitted stone finish on both the walls and ceiling. Visitors now feel as if they've descended into a cavern carved from rock, an ambiance perfect for savoring fine wine.

wine tasting room proved to be the perfect fit for this tiny 'x8' space since its only other practical use would have been orage.

hese before photos give just a hint of the dank and dreary asement. The cinderblock walls were filthy and smelled mildew. The 6 1/2 ft high ceiling made the room feel austrophobic.

roper preparation of the walls was critical to ensure the nish would wear over the years. A bleach wash destroyed ny mildew, but as the basement is two- thirds underground, certain amount of moisture naturally permeates through the ock. As an additional precaution, we used Dry-loc moisture ealing paint mixed with an anti-mildew paint additive. Paint purri P by Scentco gave the room a soft vanilla scent, which ill last up to 6 months.

Close-up of pitted stone finish

Adrienne applies Kelly King's signature "pitted stone" finish, (a 7-layer troweled-on finish made up of Aqua Finishing Solutions™ AquaColors™, Texture Coat™, SandStone™, PlasterTex™, Old world Veneziano™, and a tinted petroleum wax). While time consuming, this is a fun finish to apply and looks remarkably like real stone.

The mini-can lights seemed too modern for the old world feel of the room, This problem was resolved by adding composite ornamentation by Beaux-Artes wit a Pro-Sandstone finish by Pro Faux

It isn't necessary to spend a fortune to have a lovely mural. This paper mural was ordered on line from muralsyourway.com

This wall, painted by Susie Goldenberg and Erick Whiteside of PAINTIN' THE TOWN, FAUX , mimics an aged and weathered wine label sign. The name "Westover Winery" honors the quaint Westover neighborhood where the house is located.

44

The "tumbled marble" countertop looks so real that the contractor chided us for tiling over plywood rather than cement board. This finish was originated by Wanda Timmons, famous for her inventive countertop finishes. She applied the finish right over plywood by using a combination of texture products by Faux Effects® International, Inc. After applying a prime coat of Texture Coat™ followed by SandStone™, Wanda taped off the "grout lines" with ¼" tape. She used a combination of Olde World Marmorino™ and Olde World Veneziano™ plasters to build up the tile, then used sea salt and her trowel to distress the edges and add texture. Each tile was painted in slightly different tones then topped with C-500 Super Urethane TopCoat to ensure the countertop would hold up to entertaining.

This Textured faux "cabinet" by Michael Gross hides a water turnoff valve.

Mary and her mother Ann Kingslan are both known for their masters style still lifes. A trompe L' oeil "note" painted on the door announces wine tasting hours

This mural by Mary Gabilisco appears to lead into a wine storage room. The mural was painted with a unique medium called heat set oils. These paints (and your brushes) will stay wet for months, allowing time to work wet on wet.. Alternatively, a painting can be quickly finished by setting the paint with a special heat gun or oven.

This "aged" floor in earth tones has a warm feel and is a vast improvement over the pitted grey cement in the before photos. Susie Goldenberg and Erick Whiteside used Bella Vernici Architectural Concrete cement primer and stains with a Modello™Designs floor pattern to create this one-of-a-kind floor, perfect for a wine cellar.

Muriatic acid was used to remove stain from the design areas.

46

…aux stained glass is by muralist and faux finisher, Kate Nagle. She used acrylic …mulated liquid leading to form the outline. Once dry, she applied Plaid acrylic …allery Glass paints for the colors in layers until she got the look she wanted.

…nexpensive pine wine storage cubes were …ained to look like rich mahogany

Before

What appears to be a rustic wooden wine barrel is actually a recycled plastic industrial barrel painted by Annie Lemarié, of Main Street Arts. She used a special plastic primer to ensure adhesion and did an incredibly convincing job of wood graining the barrel. She also created a realistic "slate" top by cutting a circle from wood scrap and topping it with LusterStone™.

Maggie O'Neill and her team painted the stairwell to the basement around the wine cellar theme. A contractor added drywall to close in the left side of the steps and Maggie then wood grained the drywall and the stairs

A trompe l' oeil cork and wine glass are painted on the stairs

Maggie and her team imbedded wine corks and labels into Briste Group's Versiplast for the upper landing.

Before

Artists

Adrienne van Dooren- Room Captain, design, pitted stone and faux leather

Celeste Stewart- Room Lieutenant and wine racks

Susie Goldenberg and Erick Whiteside: stained cement floor and wine label mural

Annie Lemarié:faux wood wine barrel

Kate Nagle-faux stained glass

Michael Gross-trompe l'oeil wine cabinet

Wanda Timmons: faux tumbled marble countertop

Mary Kingslan Gibilisco- trompe l'oeil mural

Rebecca Hotop: painted glass holder

Ann Bayer-staging

Team Members: Lisa Turner, Anne Bayer, Robin Bear, Hector Lopez, Rebecca Hotop, Tracie Weir, Debbie Dennis, Carol Patterson, & Mitch Eanes

Basement Stairwell and Faux Inlaid Wood Door:

Maggie O'Neill: Project Captain/Primary Artist

Stacy Matarese-Project Lieutenant

Team Member- Christine Barnette

Room Captain Adrienne van Dooren and Room Lieutenant Celeste Stewart celebrate with a glass of wine.

Sponsors

Arlington Paint and Decorating Center-painting supplies and acid

Beaux- Artes-decorative moldings

Bella Vernici Architectural Concrete-cement overlay stain products

Colorwheel- Versiplast by Briste Group

Dominion Floors-sealing stairs

Faux Effects® International-plasters, texture products and tools

Faux Fingers-trowels

Faux Like a Pro-wax

Genesis Heat Set Oils-used in trompe l'oeil mural

Kelly S. King-invented pitted stone and aged leather finishes

Kingslan-Gabilisco Studios-heat set oils

Krylon®-plastic primer

Murals your way™ -wine country mural inside arch

Nash Timber Corp. -plastic industrial barrel

Paintin The Town Faux-Westover mural and floor products

Pro Faux® -sandstone used on moldings

Rockland Industries - Roc-lon Multi-purpose Cloth canvas for arch mural

The Mad Stencilist Embellishments Say What? - "say what" stencil

Modello Designs™-decorative masking pattern for concrete floor design

Scentco™ -vanilla scented paint additive

Stencil Planet-stencil for faux inlaid wood door

Steve Brown Construction-light installation

Artist Julie Miles took a room that was small and claustrophobic and turned it into the favorite room in the house. This long basement room had extremely low ceilings (6 1/2 feet). The white walls and trim made the room uninviting, and the lack of any windows made it dark and claustrophobic. The transformation was dramatic. The room now feels lighter, the ceilings higher and folks want to sit and stay a while—proving once again that life is too short for white walls!

Gentleman's Room

The Gentleman's Quarters is intended to be a place where a man can feel at home —to relax by a fire with a cognac and cigar.

The drywall was wood grained to resemble a rich walnut. Inset panels of faux aged leather were created using Lincrusta with hand painted details, finished with a patina glaze. Upholstery nail strips were nailed on to set the panels apart from the faux wood.

The low ceiling was painted black to make it disappear. Ceiling lights were replaced with sconces as up lighting always makes a ceiling appear taller.

Before

Trompe L'oeil details were painted by Tania Seabock to give the illusion of true 3-D moldings.

The grouse, painted in acrylics on cambric cloth, was applied to wall with wall paper glue, allowing for additional trompe l' oeil elements. Painting by Julie Miles.

These in progress shots illustrate the creation of the paneled wood grained room.

The ceiling was first painted black, then panels added. Originally, the team planned to attach antiqued mirrors to the ceiling but after hanging several they discovered the mirrors made the ceiling feel lower and too modern for the room. The panels were then pulled down and the ceiling left black, a surprisingly effective look.

The antique leather look was accomplished by purchasing Lincrusta, applying a base coat, then enhancing each panel with hand painted details. Once dry, the process was completed with a chalky patina glaze.

The wood graining is accomplished in 3 coats—here Julie applies the flog coat to provide texture and depth. The use of oils meant an exceptional luminosity to the faux wood.

Artists

Julie Miles and Brad Duerson - Room Captains
Tania Seabock - Artistic Designer /wood-grained
  Trompe l' oeil molding
Mau Don Nuyen and Nancy AtLee -Furnishings/Decor
Team Members: Hector Lopez, Ian Seabock, Celeste
Stewart, Ann Bayer, Linda O'Neal, Barb Tise, Lisa Turner,
Tracy Weir and Carol Patterson

Sponsors

Oriental Rugs and More - Leesburg VA Corner Outlets
  Hand-made in India by Sphinx, Oriental Weavers.
Golden Paints
Arlington Paints and Decorating
The Store House Furniture

Basement Bathroom

The bath was originally plumbed but never finished as a bath. It primarily held the washer, dryer and a long cement sink. Reconfigured for convenience and function it is now a usable and fun space.

Artist Jne' Medellin, VA created a Greek bath using her unique method of painting with Venetian plaster using tiny trowels. She used Modello™ adhesive stencils for her designs, completed on Roc-lon and then attached on-site. Jne' blended the attached panels into the wall with additional plaster. The panels resemble inlaid stone yet are blended and shaded in a way that mimics fresco. Jne' also covered the ceiling and floor in the same plaster for a seamless finish.

Jne' chose a frameless glass shower which essentially disappears making the room seem larger. The glass bowl sink resembles cracked glass and takes up far less room than a traditional sink. Unfortunately when installed, the contractor used white plastic PVC pipe. Celeste Stewart solved this problem by applying plastic primer and a bronze metallic paint.

A fun surprise is the Trompe l'oeil woman "caught" in just her towel painted by Machyar Gleuenta.

Artists

Jne' Medellin - Room Captain/Walls
Elizabeth T. Lee - Room Lt/Venetian Plaster Floor
Machyar Gleuenta - Mural
Team Members: Celeste Stewart and Mitch Eanes

Sponsors

Behr Venetian Plaster-plasters
Faux Effects® International-basecoat and bronze metalics
Faux fingers-miniature trowels
Noland Plumbing-sink and fixtures
Modello Designs™ - decorative masking pattern
Roc-lon-canvas Trompe l'oiel

Hall closets need not be boring; they make a great pallet for fun finishes!

This hall closet by Carol Patterson combines several techniques that add texture and interest to an otherwise boring space. Crumpled tissue paper applied to the walls with paint add interesting texture. Lusterstone and lace technique is used on the door and stencils create fun elements throughout.

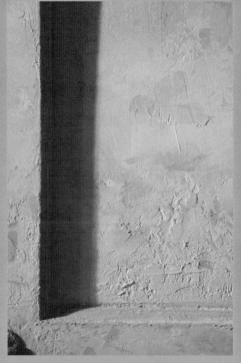

Artist Lisa Turner used O'villa™ Plaster to add an interesting texture to the inside of the hall closet and pressed in rubber fern stamps for an interesting backdrop to the birdhouse display. She useda combination of Shimerstone™ and Orastone™ products on the door.

Parvati Texture Cotton Plaster with sparkling gold and silver filaments wc hand applied creating a beautiful wall that is soft to the touch.

The rear wall of the closet was finished in a lime based Safra™ marmarino by Ian Seabock.

This trompe l'oeil door panel by Josh Yagelberg provides a fun surprise as one opens the closet door.

Small Spaces

This close-up shows the beauty of the Venetian plaster. To obtain this effect, 3-5 layers of plaster are tightly troweled and burnished to a shine. The walls appear to have texture and depth yet are smooth to the touch.

Artists

Shawn Bessenyei - Half bath
Lisa Turner - Upper hall "fern" closet
Carol Patterson - upper hall "tissue paper" closet
Tracie Weir - downstairs bath
Josh Yavelberg - closet surprise mural
Susie Goldenberg - Parvati Texture Cotton Plaster

Sponsors

Andreae Stencils - trowels and tools
Behr - Pearlescent paint
Color Wheel - Modern Masters paints and Oikos plasters
Faux Effects® International - tissue paper, Aquastone™, Lusterstone™ and
*   Irridecent Venetian Gem™ Golden - Irredecent colors*
Highlight™ colors
Jan Dressler - stencil for shoes & mannequin & adhesive vinyl floor design
Plaza Artes - metalics
Paintin the Town Faux - Parvti Texture
Stencil Planet - Angel Stencils
School of Italian Plasters - Safra™ marmarino
Finishes:
Gary Lord - teaches abalone shell finish
Kelly King - teaches finish and Lusterstone™ and lace
Melanie Royals - teaches raised stencil under tissue paper

The walls, window coverings and décor are sophisticated. But as visitors enter the shed, they discover that the back wall has been "ripped open" exposing a beautiful rolling landscape, a sweet cow, and a charismatic pig. The scene was first painted on Roc-lon cloth in the artist's studio and then attached to the wall with heavy duty wallpaper paste. This process is increasingly popular as clients prefer not to have the artist underfoot for weeks and want the option to take the art with them when they move. The edges of the canvas can be made to blend seamlessly into the wall with the use of drywall mud, so the mural looks as if it were painted directly onto the wall.

Shed & Office

The Faux House was too small to include a home office, a near necessity in today's world. The only other space available was an old storage shed. Room Captain Mary Steingesser decided to convert the exterior shed into an office with a botanical artist's theme. She wanted to make it a fun and whimsical, yet elegant. Not an easy combination to pull off, but she did it!

A donkey looks in through a faux window. The mural was painted on Roc-on by Fracesa Spingalo using a stencil by The Mad Stencilist. She then and embellished it and added shadows. The illusion becomes even more onvincing once real window molding around the outer edges and curtains dd a third dimension.

he reason for the torn wall appears to be this mischievous little pig vrapped in the "torn wallpaper." Denise Malueg painted the pig in paper sing a stencil from the Mad Stencilist.

Even the exterior of the shed was transformed from dull burgundy and grey to a cheerful yellow.

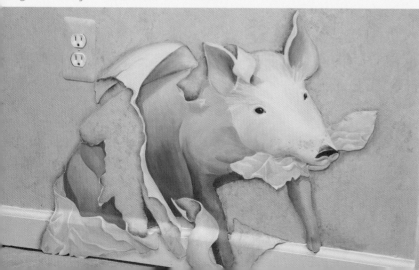

Sheri Hoeger, better known as "The Mad Stencilist" painted a trompe l'oeil "paneled" door with hanging overalls. She used an airbrush to shade the coveralls which are paint-spattered in keeping with the artist's studio theme. Sheri completed the canvas in California and shipped it to Virginia along with adhesive wax and applicator. The canvas panel was then waxed onto the existing flat wooden door, adding tons of character to the room.

Add in both elegance and interest to the ceiling is the curve of the light fixture and the one-of-a-kind ceiling medallion Mary made of hand-cast plaster.

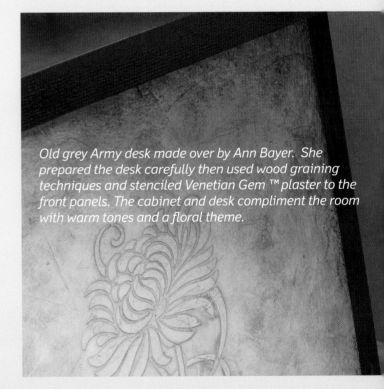

Old grey Army desk made over by Ann Bayer. She prepared the desk carefully then used wood graining techniques and stenciled Venetian Gem ™ plaster to the front panels. The cabinet and desk compliment the room with warm tones and a floral theme.

Grey Cement Floor was troweled over with skimstone™ in a pale green. The floral pattern was created with a Modello™ and skimstone tints.

Painting by Mary Steingesser

Artists

Mary Steingesser - Room Captain
Linda O'Neill - Room Lieutenant
Sheri Hoeger - Painted overalls door panel
Rose Wilde - Wood icing cabinet makeover
Francesca Springolo: Donkey in window
Anne Bayer - Desk makeover
Ceil Glemblocki - Window treatments and flower arrangements
Ashley Spencer - Trompe l' oeil shutters
Denise Malueg - pig in torn paper
Debbie Thompson - Matting and framing
Gary A - Concrete step with dog prints
Chris Jackson - Flowers for window boxes
Celeste Stewart - Exterior woodwork
Stuart Kershner - decorative moldings
Sally Skene - Mural landscape
Team Members: Lee Hickman, Ryoko Kanke, Kathy Keel, Linda Manning, Carol Rohrbaugh, Jacky Shaw, Sally Skene, Jenny Vanier-Walker, Eric of Paintin the town Faux, Carl Bayer, Rachel Steingesser, Tracie Wier, Barb Tise, Marc Steingesser, Jennifer Skene, Tania Seabock, Ann Cook, Susan Guarino, Patrick O'Neill.

... dilapidated metal cabinet was saved from the ...crapheap by Rose Wilde using Wood Icing ™

Before

Sponsors

The Mad Stencilist - Donkey and floral stencils, Daige Pro-cote waxer and adhesive wax
Wood Icing
Modello Designs™ - decorative masking pattern
Faux Effects® International
The Color Wheel
Skimstone
Golden paints
Hanging Treasures
Calico Corners
ArtStuf
Stencil Planet
Andreae Stencils
Keepmypet.com
Roc-lon
SALI - Capital Area Decorative Painters

63

The most dramatic change came from the faux brick treatment by DC Concrete Technologies.
They taped off and sprayed the finish right over the existing concrete walk.
The new look is fresh and colorful.

Photo by Omar Salinas

64

Exterior

The front entrance provides the first impression of your home. The Faux house entrance screamed "dated". We considered painting the house white or applying dyebrick products to make the brick multi-toned, but time and weather did not cooperate. In the end we decided just to show how simple changes can make a big difference.

Before

Before

Landscaper- Chris Jackson removed and transplanted the front yard's overgrown bushes and replaced them with smaller azaleas and colorful phlox. Two tall holly bushes were chosen to frame the front steps. Chris then rounded the yard's strait lines for a softer more welcoming appearance.

Volunteers painted the grey shutters black for greater contrast against the red brick. The dilapidated wooden banisters were replaced with black iron and the white plastic light was replaced with a stylish, yet inexpensive lantern style from Home Depot.

65

The side entrance was truly an eyesore with a metal awning and rusty storm-door. We removed the awning and storm door and added wood trim. Carolyn Blahosky painted a lovely country scene on canvas panel in her PA studio and later glued in into the door panel. She also stenciled the door and created wooden flower panels to hide the open storage area under the porch.

The entrance was half wooden deck/half cement stoop. The mismatched wood/cement and wood/iron rail created quite a design challenge. Cement specialist Dan Mahlmann had a brainstorm—to create faux wood from cement to tie the two materials together. He and Gary Arvanitopulos used various cement overlay products and tints to create the look and texture of wood, right down to the grain, knots and joints. Within this faux wood frame, they created a faux stone inlay with a "carved" medallion. This look was accomplished by using a Modello™ vinyl adhesive design over the 1st black layer and then applying the lighter layer of cement over it. Once the Modello was pulled out, the image appeared to be carved into the stone. The steps now resemble stone even down to the mica flakes. The wooden deck was stained in black to further blend the space.

Before

efore

The house really had no landscaping to speak of. The grass met the walkway and driveway and the shed looked —well— like a shed, making the space seem utilitarian. Landscaper Chris Jackson created a private retreat by using shrubs and plants to form a boundary for the yard and separate it from the walk and gravel drive. His use of curves softened the existing harsh geometric shapes of the house, brick walk, and patio. Chris also added a stone path connecting the two brick patio areas. Finally, window boxes, patio pots and hanging plants added both color and character.

Gary Arvanitopulos of PA created this one of a kind fountain out of lightweight materials covered in concrete. The "stone" is incredibly realistic. Gary used color variations copied from real stone and pressed in an occasional shell impression for a fossil look. The fountain represents New Orleans, with the people helping one another to rise out of the water and rubble of the hurricane to reach toward the sky of a new tomorrow. The calming sound of the waterfall makes the back yard a true oasis from a hectic world.

hoto by Omar Salinas

Stewart Kershner applied a very thin foam insulation and wood panel to cover the bead board paneling. He then glued a Beaux-Artes molding piece top and bottom for a beautiful carved wood look. He added composite molding pieces to the upper 3 panels for balance.

The addition of one of their specialty doorknob ornaments over the existing inexpensive knobmakes the door very elegant indeed.

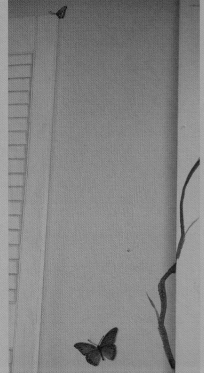

Butterflies painted by Ashley Spencer symbolize the rebirth of New Orleans

Before

Carol Farley of MD took on the challenge of making over the rusty, dented mailbox. She primed and painted the mailbox a cheerful blue, then attached mirrors and broken ceramics for a fun mosaic pattern complete with house numbers. She also added whimsical flowers, teacup handles and even a little bird to tie in with our birdhouse theme.

Artists

Celeste Stewart - Project Captain
Chris Jackson - Landscaper
Ann and Carl Bayer - Birdhouse Screen
Ashley Spencer - Trompe L' oeil Shutters
Barb Tise - Color consultant
Carol Farley - Mailbox
Carolyn Blahosky - Side entrance artwork
Dan Mahlmann and Gary Arvanitopulos -
  Concrete side porch and Shed entrance
DC Concrete technologies team: Justin Velez-
  Hagan, Russell Sellineer, Reginald Fleming, and
  Lewis Lewis
Dennis Nash - Side entrance molding
Gary Arvanitopulos - Ode to New Orleans
  fountain

Skip Calvert and Dorothy Schmitt - Landscape
  design consultants
Stuart Kershner - Decorative moldings
Suzanne Leedy - Photos and bottle sculpture

Sponsors

Action Iron - Iron Railings
Arlington Paints and Decorating Center -
  Exterior paints and brushes
Benjamin Moore - exterior paints and primers
Beaux-Artes - decorative moldings, hinge
  ornaments and doorknob surrounds
Chris Jackson Landscaping
Andrea Stencils - Birdhouse stencils for tri - screen
Color Alchemist School & Restoration - exterior
  painting
Colesville Nursery - Holly plants
DC Concrete Technology - Front entrance concrete

Decorative Concrete of Maryland, Inc.
Decorator's Supply - Composite moldings
Faux Effects® International - Mica flakes and stain
Golden Paints - Painted Planters and artist's colors
Home Depot - Exterior lighting
Krylon Paints - Primers / black paint for iron rails
Modello Designs™ - decorative masking pattern
Royal Design Studio - Side window stencils
Stencilworks - Stencils for door and wooden panels
Mad Stencilist - Stencils for the exterior of the shed
Priscilla Hauser - Birdhouse idea books
Pure Texture Concrete - Fountain materials
Red Lion Stencils - Stencil
Restoration Hardware - Fire pit
Roc-Lon
Thompson Creek Windows - Bay window
Wing Enterprises - Little Giant Ladder™

69

Church of the Atonement

The Church of the Atonement was founded in by a 1886 a group of Episcopalian families who met in a building at Bryn Mawr and Winthrop Avenues. In November 1888, the group became a Mission of the diocese to be known as The Church of the Atonement. The cornerstone of the original Church was laid in November of 1889 at the present site at Kenmore and Ardmore. Expanded several times the church maintained it's original character. The Christ the King window in the North Chapel has been recognized as one of the best in Chicago. Father John David van Dooren became rector in August 2006 after spending the majority of his ministry at All Souls Church in Washington, D.C. He found his new church and rectory had beautiful lines and architectural elements, but over the years they had either deteriorated or had simply been painted white. When the House that Faux Built Project became too large for the Arlington House, the church and rectory provided an excellent pallet for the additional artisans.

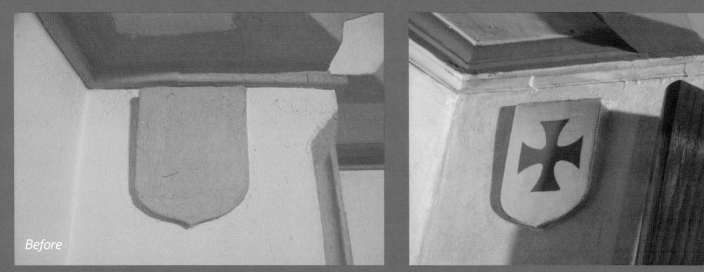

Before

The narthex walls were painted to replicate stone blocks.

Lime-based plaster was used to cover the flaking ceiling panels which were then hand-painted with a leaf design.
The moldings were gold-leafed to add dimension and reflect the character of the church.

The english crosses were painted over silver-leafed shield backgrounds.

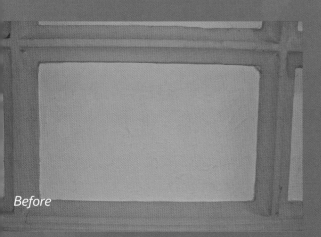

Before

This entry leading to the fellowship hall and church offices was not in the original faux plan. However, Chicago artists Chesna Koch and Sue Sidun felt the entrance would be the perfect place to hang the domed ceiling Gicle' by Yves Lantheir. Once hung, it was apparent the ceiling needed glazing and aging…which made the wall look too white. Glazing the walls in a slightly lighter version of the ceiling color provided warmth and made the cinderblock resemble stone block. The ugly bulletin board just didn't fit in with this new look, so Adrienne painted it black and attached Beaux-Artes moldings to make it look more like art. All of this was done in just one day!

Printed canvases are a cost effective way for homeowners to add beautiful art to their walls and ceilings. Heavier canvases require heavy-duty wall paper glue and several people to apply to a ceiling or can be installed by a wall paper professional.

74

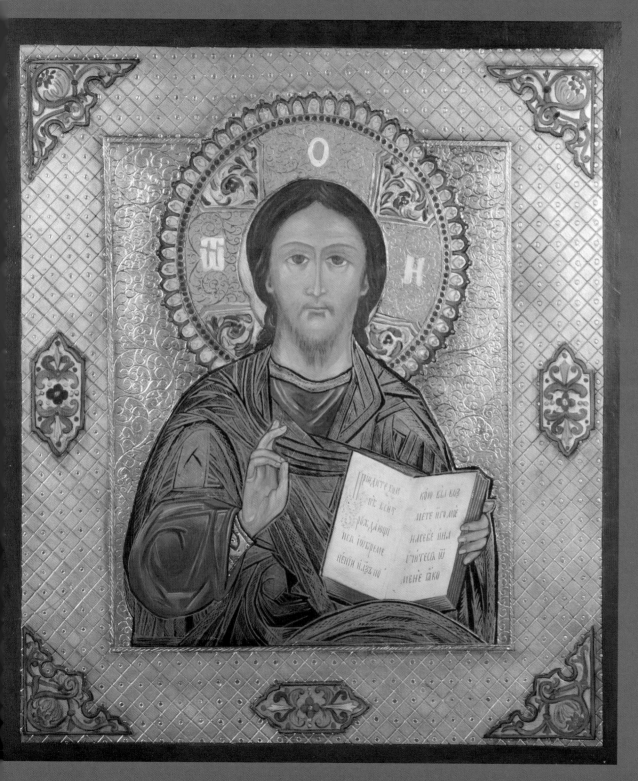

Icon by Tania Seabock using traditional methods

Artists

Gicle' mural by Jeff Ingram and Brian Townsend
Faux marble floor cloth by Leonard Pardon
Team members: Maciej Adamek, Maros Koncok,
Miroslav Sebestik

Sponsors

Beaux-Artes - Moldings
Roc-lon cloth - Floorcloth canvas
The Mad Stencilist - Mounting wax and Daige
   Waxer
Faux Effects® International
Easy Leaf
Zinsser products

Visitors of all faiths are welcome to attend mass
and see the artwork in this chapter:
5749 North Kenmore Avenue • Chicago, IL 60660
Phone: 773-271-2727 • Fax: 773-271-4295
e-mail: info@ChurchOfTheAtonement.org
www.ChurchOfTheAtonement.org

Dining Room

Rectory

The Rectory's large formal dining room is used 2-3 times a week for church dinners, meetings and entertaining. The large wall panels had been painted with contrasting trim but were simply lost on the wall. Gary Lord, author of It's Faux Easy, used his signature foil sheets and lace to create these beautiful glimmering panels. Assisted by Kathy Carroll and her students from the Chicago Institute of Fine Finishes, they used size followed by multicolored foils of pale blue, pink, silver and gold. To crate the floral pattern, Gary carefully selected a lace to complement the room's elegant décor. He then taped up the lace and troweled Lusterstone™ thru it to create the look of needlepoint. The lace panels can be washed, air dried and reused several times.

This before photo shows how bland the room looked before Gary used his foil technique to finish the panels.

Before

Study

Artist Paulette Piazza hanged the rectory study from plain white walls to old world style in only 2 days. The room was first painted a williamsberg green. Then a canvas map added and fauxed into the wall.

Adrienne van Dooren fauxed over plain black bar with cheesecloth, plasters and wax to create a masculine looking snakeskin effect

Before

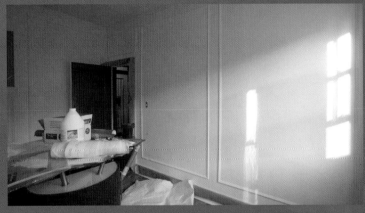

An extra bedroom in the rectory was changed into a child's guest room for little god- daughter Anna who frequently visits from Washington, D.C. The Williamsburg grey walls were far too solemn for a 3 year old, and the small child's bed was lost under the high paneled walls. Artist Paulette Piazza decided to brighten the room with white paint and accessories. She then matched the bright pastels of the bedspread and painted each panel trim a different color with Golden acrylics™. While an accomplished mural artist, Paulette loved the ease of the princess stage drape transfer by Elephant's on the Wall. Easy enough for even the artistically impaired, each kit comes with the full size pattern, transfer/ carbon paper, instructions and a color guide, making it as easy as paint by the numbers. Paulette decided to deviate from the list of recommended colors in order to match the colors in the bedspread. She also decided against painting "princess" or Anna's name as recommended inside the name plaque so that the room could host other visitors with children. Instead, she recommended a set of wooden letters to personalize the room to the visitor. One doesn't have to be a child to feel like a princess in this room!

These darling animals, also completed from an Elephants on the Wall transfer, were painted by Kacki Berri and Emily Cato in Washington DC on Roc-lon cloth. Paulette and Adrienne then simply cut them out and pasted them on the wall for a whole new look. Once Anna outgrows the design, the animals can be removed.

Artists

Gary Lord - Dining Room
Paulette Piazza - Kid's Room and Study
Kacci Berry - Kids animals for bath
Adrienne van Dooren - Snakeskin Bar and Stairwell
Nicola Vigini - Grotesca panels for stairwell
Yves Lanthier - Canvas panel-study
Patti Newton - Designed Elephants on the Wall
    transfers
Team Members: Kacki Berri, Chesna Koch, Sue
Sidun, Kathy Carrol and class

Sponsors

Elephants on the Wall-transfers for kids room
Faux Effects® International
Golden Paints
Prismatic Studios - Foils
Pro Faux
The Faux School
Roc-lon

Before

William Cochran

William Cochran also does exterior trompe l' oeil for which he is best known

Michel Nadaï

Patricia Buzzo
and partner Andreas

Tania Seabock

Josh Yagelberg

Pierre Finkelstein, Sean Crosby, Pascal Amblard and Nicola Vigini

Karen Derrico

Adrienne van Dooren

Pascal Amblard and Sean Crosby

Adrienne van Dooren

Pascal Amblard and Sean Crosby

Carol van Gerena

Karen Derrico with screen by Michael Gross

84

donated mural by Randy Ingram and Brian Townson
is perfectly complemented by a painted "inlay marble"
floorcloth by Leonard Pardon. Together they transform
a dingy bath in the Chicago Church Project

Beaux- Artes Moldings glued over canvas onto wall make canvas panel look like a large framed painting

Floorcloth below by Leonard Pardon
was donated for Habitat auction

85

Sherrie Hoeger

Julie Miles

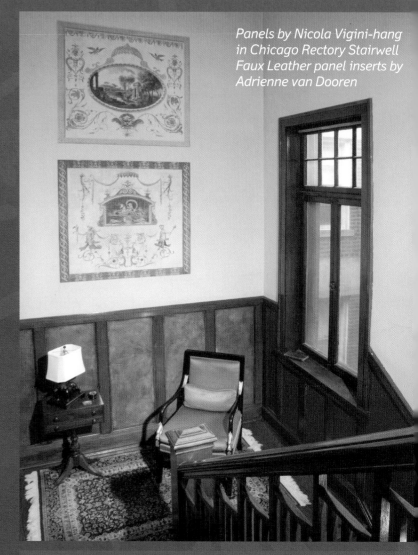

Panels by Nicola Vigini-hang
in Chicago Rectory Stairwell
Faux Leather panel inserts by
Adrienne van Dooren

Artists
See photo credits

Sponsors
Golden Paints
Roc-lon
Modello Designs™ -
   decorative masking pattern
Faux Effects® International
Mad Stencilist
Hanging Treasures
Johnie Liliandahl

Furniture

Kelly King teaches furniture makeovers in his Omaha studio. He remade this old piece using crackle and gold leaf.

Furniture for the Romantic Bedroom

Joanne's husband, Dennis made the single bed and fireplace for the romantic bedroom. The fireplace was made of scrap wood and the hearth from masonite board. The headboard is made of simple MDF board and table legs. Joanne used steam-on composite ornamentation by Decorators Supply on both the headboard and an old humidor table to make them appear to be matched pieces. She then primed and painted both cream adding touches of brown paint to distress the finish.

An old chair found in the trash finds a new life.

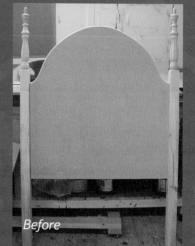

Before

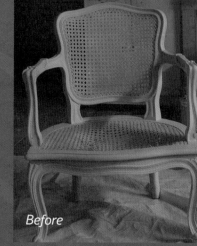

Before

Armoire makeover by Joanne Nash

Kitchen Furniture

wooden trash can was built by Michael Gross specifically to fit with the Italian theme of the Arlington *itchen*. Michael used art transfers (imprints™) made by Faux Effects® International, then aged and distressed it for an old world look.

atti Irwin used casein paints for this $10 yard sale table makeover for the Arlington kitchen.

her casein, (milk paint) style furniture makeovers.

Shireen Balkissoon

Patti Irwin

Luba Marx

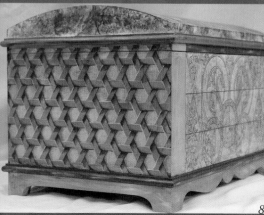

Having Fun with Furniture

Patty Irwin adds fun to unfinished furniture

Trompe l'oeil Banana Shipment chest by Jeff Monsein

Before

Kathleen Sakry updated an old piece by painting it in a faux burl and adding trompe l' oeil molding and butterflies.

Painted furniture can be repainted to look like wood.

Artists
See photo credits

Sponsors
Golden Paints
Roc-lon
Modello Designs™ -
   decorative masking pattern
Faux Effects® International
Mad Stencilist
Hanging Treasures
Johnie Liliandahl

Cheri Perry

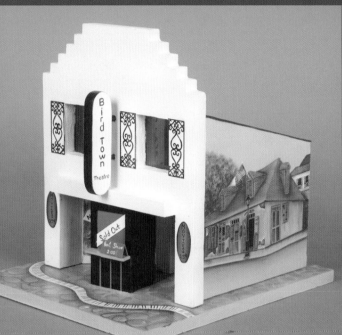

Donna Busch

Kathi Ryan-Reagan

Audrey Nepper

Becky Peterson

Ann Bayer

Carol Farley

Debbie Brown

Debra Maerz

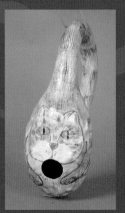

Faye Davis

Gina Dearaway

Joyce Ann Clark

Sammie Crawford

Cheryl King

The Birdhouse Contest ensured that artists from across the U.S./ overseas could play a role in the House that Faux Built Project.

Artists were asked to submit birdhouses "any shape, any size" either fauxed or painted It seemed appropriate that these "houses" will help find homes for feathered and furry survivors of hurricanes.

We were amazed both at the number of submissions--and the talent, creativity and effort evident in each birdhouse. It was impossible to choose only 30 for inclusion in the book, therefore, also pictured are honorable mentions

A selected birdhouse was donated to go with the house that faux built. The others were auctioned locally and on Ebay with 100% of proceeds to raise money for Noah's Wish Animal Charity. Those who wish to support or learn more about this important charity can read more at: www.noahswish.org.
Donations can be made on line by credit card or mailed directly to: Noah's Wish, P.O. Box 997, Placerville, CA 95667

Jean Schettler

Judith A. MacLaren

Resident Mockingbird

Judy Luchino

June Yovanovich

Kathryn Leonard

Kerry Trout

Judy Krebs

Judy Yett

Linda Hoerner

Linda Kinnaman

Lorena M. Vicente

Patricia Hauser

Louise Kramer

Sammie Crawford

Sandra Weiner

Sherry A. Barnett

Suzanne Leedy

Annemairé Caola

Dorie Wilson

Gina Dearaway

Jenny Vanier-Walter

Jonie Bassie

94

Joyce Moore

Kande McBride

Kathleen Hoegard

Laurin

Mary B. Walberg

Nalini Keshav

Pricilla Hauser

Terri M. Bayer

S. Colgain

Susan Rensch

Bernice Dupré

Kate Hill

Artists

Gary Arvanitopulos:
Born and raised in Greece, Argirios "Gary" Arvanitopulos has a natural talent in creating magnificent finishes. Owner of Exquisite Finishes located in Erie, PA, Gary boasts over 20 years experience in decorative painting. He began in Jewelry Fabrication and later expanded to with faux finishes and fine furniture. He has trained with experienced professionals in Mastering faux marbling, wood graining, gilding, glazing, old world finishes, as well as extensive training in decorative concrete techniques. His combination of European and American culture, experience and training allows the creation of beautiful faux finish and decorative concrete masterpieces. His work is characterized by imagination and creativity Argirios' work on the Arlington project includes the design and creation of the outside waterfall, concrete modello, landing, shed, entrance and concrete countertop in the kitchen.
www.exquisite-finishes.com

Pascal Amblard:
Pascal Amblard, France, specializes in trompe l'oeil and teaches internationally. His work was exhibited in the biggest international decoration show in Paris: Maison et Objet. Pascal often guest teaches at US studios and serves as a co-instructor for Vigini Studio's annual Italy Trip/Class. He contributed trompe l'oeil elements to the mural "Indian woman in the window" located in the master bedroom, and was the primary artist for the "seascape" mural located in the Chicago Church. Pascal's work is internationally known and he has been invited to participate in the International SALON of Decorative Painting since 1998 and hosted it in 2001. His work has been displayed in many prestigious shows to include the Museum of Trompe L'Oeil, Perigueux.
www.crosby-amblard-studios.com

Ann Bayer:
Ann Bayer, owner of Faux and Fleur Design Arlington, VA, partners with her husband, Carl to offer decorative finishes for both residential and commercial clients. She has a studio display house where, by appointment, potential customers and designers can actually see and touch many finishes on a variety of surfaces. She and Carl frequently travel the US for commissioned work. Due to Ann's superior finishing expertise and business sense, she was selected as Vice-Chair for Project Oversight and Hospitality. Ann served as Room Captain for the living room and painted a table, desk and the decorative wooden birdhouse screen for the Arlington project.
FauxandFleur@aol.com

William Cochran:
William Cochran has worked as a professional muralist for twenty years. A trompe l'oeil master and teacher, most of his work is designed for American downtowns. Public Art Review has called him "one of America's leading muralists." His immense attachment to the community shows in his touching streetscape work. His art has won numerous national awards, including the Project of the Year award from the International Association for Public Participation (2001), the Project of the Year award from the American Public Works Association (1999) for Community Bridge, and the Award for Excellence from the American Glass Association. Mr. Cochran has been called "a born teacher," He has donated the owl mural to the Chicago project.
www.WilliamCochran.com

Sean Crosby:
Sean Crosby is a self-taught artist with over 20 years experience. He began his professional career as a union bridge painter for the City of New York, and soon became the city's head instructor of painted decoration. Sean's projects have included the Russian Tea Room in New York City, the New York apartment of film stars Michael Douglas and Catherine Zeta-Jones, and the home of Hollywood director Michael Caton-Jones, and his work has appeared in numerous highly-regarded national publications. He and Pascal Amblard own the Crosby-Amblard Studio in Delaware and one of the nation's highest regarded schools of mural, trompe l'oeil, graining and marbling. He contributed painted mural panels to both HTFB projects.
www.crosby-amblard-studios.com

Karen Derrico:
Animals may not speak in real life, but for Karen Derrico they speak volumes on canvas. Using vivid colors and dimensional brush strokes in a semi-impressionistic style, Karen's artwork is created exclusively with advanced digital painting tools. However, hers is anything but push-button artistry. Karen starts with a blank "canvas" and paints stroke by stroke to create her artwork, using photographs as a reference. Karen's talent for bringing animals to life through her art is gaining widespread recognition. Karen is founder of Painting 4 Paws which has raised more than $10,000 for animal charities around the country. Karen donated the Westie painting and sleeping dog mural to the Arlington project.
www.painting4paws.com

Deborah Drager:
Deb Drager owns Drager Design Studio and is the Director of ART-i-MATRIX Academy of Architectural Finishes, Wichita, KS. She is also a leading distributor of the Coral-lite™ products, which have completely transformed the HTFB master bath, Arlington Project. Deb has a BFA in Fine Art and is a seasoned faux finisher, instructor, and graphic designer. Her original faux designs have been featured in several magazines and she was hired by Faux Effects® International to create marketing tools for the corporation and networks schools/artisans. In addition to the bath, Deb assisted in the design of the book.
www.ddrager.com

Brad Duerson:
Brad Duerson has a vast background of experience in historical restoration and building, including carpentry, tin-smithing (nearly a lost art), and masonry. >He is also very accomplished in the decorative painting field. In addition to painted wall finishes he specializes in plasters, such as Venetian, and old world and marmorino. He and his wife Julie worked as a team on the basement floor Arlington project. Brad did lighting, drywall work, built in the fireplace and assisted in the faux finishing. He also gave the male perspective on what should be included in the "gentlemen's room"
www.jmilesstudios.com

Pierre Finkelstein:
Pierre Finkelstein is known internationally for his faux wood and marble techniques and tools. A published author and renowned instructor, he is a long-time member of Salon and a 1986 Gold Medal graduate of the Van Der Kellen Painting Institute in Brussels. Pierre was awarded the distinguished title of "Best Craftsman In France" for decorative painting by the French Government in 1990. He is the owner of Grand Illusion Decorative Painting, Inc. and has created faux finishes for internationally acclaimed interior designers and architects in Europe and the United States. He, along with Sean Crosby, Pascal Amblard and Nicola Vigini, completed the incredible Indian mural in the master bedroom and the "Hall of Ruins" mural for the Chicago church project.
www.pfinkelstein.com

Mary Kingslan Gibilisco:
Mary Kingslan Gibilisco, CDA, Omaha has had a life long interest in art. She began studying art formally in 1979 at the University of Nebraska and in 1984 graduated Magna Cum Laude with a degree in Fine Art and a minor in Art History. In 1989, she received her Certified Decorative Artists distinction. She currently partners with her Mother, Anne Kingslan, in their Omaha based studio. Mary is a superior instructor on Trompe L'oeil, realistic still lifes and the exciting new genesis heat-set oils. Her studio also carries a full line of instructional videos and booklets. Mary painted the trompe l' oeil mural for the base of the wine cellar steps, Arlington Project.
www.kingslan.com

Machyar Gleuenta:
Machyar Gleuenta was born and raised in Acheh, a northern region of Sumatra the epicenter of the deadly earthquake and subsequent tsunami of December 26, 2004. He began his career in art working as an artist's helper in Acheh and continued to follow this path when he moved to Jakarta, Indonesia. It was during this time period that his talents came to the attention of both the local and international communities.Machyar received a full scholarship from the Maine College of Art in Portland Maine. Prior to departing for the United States, officials in the United States Embassy in Jakarta, as well as businessmen in Indonesia, helped raise the funds necessary for him to make his journey to America to begin his formal studies. In addition to the Maine College of Art, Machyar also studied at the Pennsylvania Academy of the Fine Arts in Philadelphia. People often comment that his landscapes and portraits are reminiscent of the "Old Masters". MK painted the blond woman in towel in the basement bath.

Adrian Greenfield:
Adrian flew from Essex, England to participate in the House that Faux Built project. He originally trained as a painter but later discovered his passion was decorative art and murals. He now has over 10 year's experience painting Tromp L'oeil and murals, stenciling, and an extensive line of wall finishes. His works include a number of hotels, restaurants and private clients in Europe and in the US. He has been invited to participate in the International Artist Exchange 2006. Adrian's trompe L'oeil fireplace panel featuring realistic Dutch tile and faux molding above the fireplace are featured in the Arlington project's romantic bedroom.
agelin@tiscali.co.uk

Susie Goldenberg:
Susie Goldenberg is the founder and director of Paintin' the Town Faux in Atlanta, Georgia. A Master Decorative Artist, she oversees client projects; operates her retail showroom and gallery; and she teaches. Her work has been featured in decorative arts magazines, in many show houses throughout Atlanta, and is currently featured on HGTV. Susie and Eric Whiteside completed the wine cellar floor and mural-Arlington and applied her signature Parvati Textures Cotton Plaster™ product in the master bath closet.
www.paintinthetown.com

Sheri Hoeger:
Sheri Hoeger, the "Mad Stencilist" of Placerville, CA is nationally known for her airbrushed stenciling technique. She offers workshops at her studio, the National SALI convention, and premiere schools across the country. Sheri has a full line of stencils as well as the "Say What?™" custom cut lettering system. She also carries the specialty wax and applicator tool used to apply murals in the HTFB. Sheri has been featured in several books, TV, and magazines. Sheri painted the trompe l' oeil painter's overall door panel for the Shed turned Artist's Studio as well as a floor cloth for auction, She also furnished stencils and the Say What™ stencils for the upper hallway, Arlington.
www.madstencilist.com.

Randy Ingram and Bryan Townsend:
Randy studied at the DuCret School of Fine Art, while Brian studied at the National Academy of Design in New York City. Brain's portraits and still-life paintings are becoming prized Gallery collectables. Commissions include private, corporate and museum clients. Both artists are Faux-cademy award winners. Their work has been featured in Faux Effects World, The Faux Finisher, and The Journal Magazine. The team also offers mural instruction. They donated a mural on canvas to the Chicago church project.
www.classicalartstudios.com

Patti Irwin:
Owner of Taperan Studios, Patti is a multi-talented artist, but her passion lies in creating one of a kind furniture pieces. Having trained with Pierre Finkelstein, Nicola Vigini, Jean-Pierre Besenval, and Patrick Kirwin, she is proficient in trompe l 'oeil and decorative painting. Patti painted a $10 yard sale table with vines painted to mimic the window fabric in the kitchen. The drop leaf includes a Tuscan scene. for the Arlington project. Patti also serves as Vice-Chair for the overall HTFB project bringing her superior organizational and leadership skills in to play. In addition, Patti is vice-president of her local SALI chapter, the Chesapeake Bay Stencilers.
www.taperanstudio.com

Michael Gross:
Michael's Creations founder Michael Gross began faux and decorative painting in 1994. Professionally trained by the N.Y. based "The Finishing School, Inc." and "The Academy of Wall Artistry" of Fairfax, VA, he has been an award-winning student of art from an early age, Michael has used his skills to create unique atmospheres in many forms, ranging from theatrical sets to murals and custom wall finishes. In his free time Michael enjoys figurative sculpting and woodworking. Still a student of art, he continues to enhance his abilities through continued training and frequent experimentation with new techniques and materials. He then combines these skills and artistic visions with his experience as a professional painter for truly unique and beautiful "creations". Michael completed the wine cellar cabinet, fire screen for sleeping dog, and elegant wooden trashcan for the Arlington project.
www.michaelscreations.com

Artists

Amy Ketteran:
Ketteran Studios combines Amy's classical and theatrical art training. She received her BA in Studio Art from Grinnell College, and her MFA in Scenic Art from Brandeis University. Her varied training allows her to work quickly and efficiently, without sacrificing quality and individuality. She is also a highly regarded instructor. Her teaching philosophy is based on her students learning how to see, then apply this knowledge to varied mediums. Active in the Stencilist's Artisans League, Inc. (SALI), she is currently the president of the local chapter, the Chesapeake Bay Stencilers (CBS). She has also taught several classes at the SALI National Convention. Amy has completely transformed the upstairs hall and stairwell of the Arlington project.
www.ketteranstudios.com

Kelly S. King:
Kelly S. King is the owner of the Faux Finish Institute and one of the nation's top decorative artists. The Faux Finish Institute has two locations-Omaha, Nebraska and Seattle, Washington. Services include decorative wall finishes, furniture finishing, woodwork and cabinetry.
The Faux Finish Institute is one of the most unique training facilities in the world; a state of the art 6000-sqft training facility that sits behind a 14,000-sqft home called "The Painted Mansion", avail. for students to stay while they study at the Faux Finish Institute. The Painted Mansion is an ongoing work of decorative finishing art in which the students will be able to see decorative finishing in progress throughout their stay and live in the environment for which they are training. Kelly's work is featured in the book's furniture chapter. Further, two of his signature finishes will be shown in the wine cellar of the Arlington project. Kelly also hosts the Fauxcademy, a national awards event for faux finishers and decorative artists.
www.in-faux.com

Melanie Kershner:
Melanie Kershner of Heavenly Home Designs is a highly sought after and experienced faux finisher/muralist. She is also co-owner of Beaux-Artes, MD. She has many years experience in the field and is well known and respected as an expert on combining different techniques and products for a trully unique finish. She created heaven in the clouds in the children's nursery to include the 4 walls, ceiling, and floor-cloth. Her room includes minerals added to the paints to make it glow in the dark. Beaux-Artes work has been featured nationally in publications, multiple showhouses and television.
www.heavenlyhomedesigns.com

Stuart Kershner:
Stuart Kershner of Beaux-Artes, MD donated and applied architectural finishes to every room using their extensive line of architectural detailing resources These small changes made the house and church transformation complete. Beaux-Artes begins where decoration usually ends- with ceilings, pilasters, custom door and window trim, and custom fabrication services ranging from ornate plaster ceilings and architectural panels to artful grills for HVAC vents and recessed lights, to amazing cabinet make-overs. Thir decorative hinge straps
www.beauxartes.com

Chesna Koch:
Chesna Koch, of Chesna Koch Artistic Finishes, has been painting and creating decorative finishes since 1989. Chesna's work has become valued for its sophistication and timelessness.

She is currently enjoying a successful decorative arts service in Chicago, IL. She was in charge of the Chicago church grottesca stairwell and fellowship hallway. Her work and client homes have been featured in several showcase houses, Southern Accents, D Home, Dallas Home Design, Modern Luxury Dallas, and the book Spectacular Homes of Texas.
www.chesnakoch.com

Yves Lanthier:
Born in St. Jérôme, Québec, Canada, Yves Lanthier's artwork has won multiple awards. He has been profiled in numerous publications including Florida Design, Art Business News, Palm Beach Illustrated, and Boca Raton News. Named one of the World's Best Trompe L'Oeil Artists In December 2004, his commissions include multi-million dollar estates such as Celine Dion's in Jupiter, Florida. He recently published " The Art of Trompe L'Oeil Murals". Both the book and large canvas reproductions of his work are available on his website. Yves is contributed two murals to the Chicago church project.
www.yvesart.com

Ron Layman:
Ron Layman owns the Faux School, MD and in Orlando, FL and offers a wide range of instruction on all elements of faux. He also carries products to include: Rivedil™, Adicollor, MM, Mica Powders, MIXOL™, brushes, tools, sprayers, etc He often brings in guest instructors such as Barth White and William Cochran . As Room Captain for the master bedroom, Ron created a truly unique and elegant room with the theme "Crossroads to Culture" incorporating a mix of Moroccan, Moorish, Indonesian an Indian design elements.
www.thefauxschool.com

Annie Lemarié:
Annie Lemarié is the owner of Main Street Arts LLC, a decorative arts studio located in central Maryland. The company offers graining, marbling, glazed and plaster wall finishes, gilding, casting and murals, and often works in the exacting historic restoration arena. Annie trained in fine arts at the Maryland Institute College of Art in Baltimore, Maryland, and has studied with several artists and studios in the U.S. Projects have been published in Elle Décor magazine, Frederick magazine and Washington Home and Gardens magazine. Since 1980, she has been providing custom decorative arts for interior designers, architects and private clients in the mid-Atlantic region, and throughout the United States.
www.mainstreetarts.com

Dan Mahlmann:
Dan Mahlmann, owner of Decorative Concrete of Maryland, Inc. earned his master's certificate in applications from the World of Concrete in 2005. His company specializes in decorative interior and exterior concrete applications resulting in high end finishes for walks, countertops, flooring, vertical walls, even toilets! He uses overlays, decorative patterns, vertical wall textures, and acid stains as well as concrete stamping and faux rock materials to create one of a kind finishes.
www.decorativeconcreteofmd.com

Gary Lord:
Gary Lord is recognized as an international artist, teacher, author and television personality. Gary's work has recently been awarded 2 National 1st Place Awards for Best Faux Finisher of the Year Gary has been teaching over 15 years to thou-

sands of students. He believes that by operating his own decorative painting business, Gary Lord Wall Options and Associates Inc., he can better share the real "tricks of the trade" and practical business knowledge he has gained in almost 30 years with the students in each class. Gary is well known for his metallic foils and one of a kind faux finishes. He demonstrated one of his signature finishes in the Chicago Church project.
www.prismaticstudio.com

Jne' Medellin:
Jne' Medellin began her faux career with Twin Diamonds Studio, MD and traveled nationwide on commissioned projects. She later started her own company in Virginia- BG Decorative Painting Studio. Her work is featured in several local restaurants, Old Town Shops and across the US. Jne' is trained in and utilizes almost every decorative painting product line and has created several finishes which are trully unique and beautiful. She is also an accomplished muralist and will create a mural in the downstairs bath, which will be "painted" with Behr venetian plaster.
www.bgdecorativepaint.com

Julie Miles:
J Miles Studios Inc., founded in 1991, is a full service decorative painting studio serving the Washington D.C. Metropolitan area and all points beyond. Dedicated to the hands on artistry and craftsmanship of the decorative painting industry, Julie has 25 years of painting experience, a BFA from Virginia Commonwealth University, and has studied with many masters in the field. Julie is joined in the business by her husband Brad Duerson. Brad brings his natural artistic hand as well as his diverse background in historical restoration including carpentry, tinsmithing and masonry. Together they are transforming the downstairs gentlemen's game room, Arlington project.
www.jmilesstudios.com

Joanne Nash:
Joanne Nash is one of the top decorative artists in Virginia. She has been featured in several magazines and her award winning trompe l' oeil was featured at the International Artist Exchange in 2004. While her studio is in Gladys VA (near Lynchburg.), she does a great deal of commissioned work in Smith Mt Lake, Richmond, Washington, DC and California. Joanne is a favorite of top designers because she can create one of a kind signature finishes to complement any room and often brings fabric elements into hand painted wall or furniture embellishments. Having studied in Italy, she was inspired by the grotesca scroll work so popular there and has incorporated it into her custom design work for the romantic bedroom.
www.joannenash.com

Maggie O'Neill:
With a Masters of Fine Art at the University of Georgia Cortona, Italy program, Maggie was moved by the rich art history of the Renaissance. Maggie's portfolio includes exterior murals, restaurants, shops, architectural painting, commissioned fine art, portraits, and documentary photography. Her work has been featured in several show houses and exhibits and she was selected by the D.C. Commission on the Arts and Humanitiesfor the public art project; "Pandamania". She has expanded her work to include decorative consulting, production and decorative painting.
www.oneillstudios.com

Leonard Pardon:
Leonard Pardon trained as an artist then was apprenticed for 7 years to British Master- A. E. Baxby. There he learned the techniques passed through the generations since the middle ages. Leonard Pardon has through his own teaching and his step-by-step, how to videos, passed this to a new generation of students who are now successfully carrying out the work worldwide. His clientele include Kings, Queens, Sultans, Sheikhs, film and rock stars. He recently had 13 of his series of videos shown nationwide by PBS. He has appeared on Discovery Channel on Home Matters and numerous guest appearances on overseas cable channels. Leonard used marbling and wood grain techniques on two canvas floor panels.
www.pardonstudio.com

Paulette Piazza:
Paulette Piazza owns and operates her Decorative Wall Artist business in Denver, Colorado from which she serves all the surrounding Rocky Mountain resorts. Her expertise is in hand painted murals, frescoes, trompe l'oeil, all levels of original faux finishes and Italian plasters.
Her extensive experience has been obtained through St. John's University, NY, one year scholarship at the Academia Di Belle Arti in Perugia, Italy, Foreign Studies with trompe l'oeil artist Janet Shearer, England, in Italy with trompe l'oeil artist Nicola Vigini, apprenticeship with trompe l'oeil artist William Cochran and decorative painting at the finest schools in New York, Texas, Colorado, California and Maryland.
Paulette transformed the study/ library with a mural and an amazing one-of-a-kind map and created a child's dream room in Church of the Atonement in Chicago.
www.piazzartist.com

Jacek Prowinski:
As an experienced artisan, Jacek Prowinski focuses on the details while preserving the authenticity of historic structures and churches.He has a teaching degree and is a graduate of a professional painting school. He has taught all aspects of faux painting workshops ranging from one-day to five-day comprehensive training sessions. Co-owner of Faux Design Studio in Addison, Illinois, Jacek has directed crews on-site for both residential and commercial commissions. His extensive field experience enables him to empower his students with not only cutting-edge decorative finishes, but on-the-job advice and business savvy. Jacek has been profiled in a number of publications including The Faux Finisher and Profiles In Faux Finishing. He has been featured on episodes of HGTV's New Spaces program and is well known throughout Chicago and US for his church commissions. Jacek was selected to work his magic on the Chicago Chicago Church Narthex which adjoins the Sanctuary.
www.fauxdesignstudio.com

Donna Phelps
Donna Phelps is owner and principle instructor of The Sarasota School of Decorative Arts, Inc. Her style is fresh and cutting edge. She has more than 18 years of training and experience in both old world techniques and new age products which ensures her students receive a wealth of real world knowledge, technical support, and the unique opportunity to learn to execute complex finishes. Donna is a very popular instructor at the Stencil Artisan's League International conferences, the annual "Faux Event ", and is often asked to teach at other schools across the country and internationally. She is also much sought after by designers for her one of a kind finishes and her new stencil line. She completed the beautiful palm frond finish in the Master bath.
www.ssda1.com

Artists

Melanie Royals:
Melanie Royals is the President/Creative Director of Royal Design Studio, an industry leader known for creating innovative and elegant stencil designs and techniques. Her work, art and "Extraordinary Stenciled Effects" program have helped to raise stenciling to the higher level of appreciation and application that it has become today. Most recently she has taken decorative pattern application to an even broader level by introducing Modello Designs™ - decorative masking pattern, custom-sized adhesive designs that have revolutionized the industry. Melanie shares her passion and knowledge of decorative art and surface decoration through an acclaimed video series, books, workshops, television appearances and regular magazine articles.
www.royaldesignstudio.com

Tania Seabock:
Tania Seabock of Seabock Studios is a one of the most acclaimed decorative/restorative artists in the Washington D.C. metro area. She works in many mediums such as gilding, sculpting, glass, moldmaking/casting, plasters and painting. She graduated from The Nadaï-Verdon Advanced School of Decorative Painting in the southwest of France and specializes in wood grain, marble, gilding, compo and ceiling design. She works with her husband Ian who specializes in moldmaking & casting, glass, bronze, plasters.
www.seabockstudios.com

Ashley Spencer
C. Ashley Spencer grew up in the flamboyant and artistic city of New Orleans. She still has a strong connection to her hometown and is excited to help them rebuild by participation in this project. A graduate, with a degree in Art History and a minor in Fine Arts, from The University of the South, Ashley also studied at Parsons in Paris and the Corcoran Gallery of Art, in Washington, D.C. She has worked at the National Gallery of Art--Design and Installation Department, National Gallery Of Women in the Arts--Exhibition Design Department, and at Washington, D.C.'s Arena Stage as a scenic painter. She was the graphic artist and illustrator for Consumers' Research Magazine for 15 years. She attributes her success to her talented art teachers, her study and appreciation of art history and her strong background in drawing--from which every good painting derives. More information can be found on her website: www.ashley-spencer.com.

Francesca Springolo:
Francesca Springolo was born in Milan, Italy on October 9 1972. From an early age she had a great passion for painting. She graduated from the "Scuola del Fumetto" in Milan and became an illustrator. The opportunity to work on a large-scale project materialized in the spring of 1996 and since then she has traveled the world decorating restaurants, hotels and private homes in Italy, Germany, Mexico and the United States. She met her husband Geoff in Venice, Italy in the summer of 2000 and then moved to the United States, settling in Bethesda MD. Francesca completed a trompe l' oeil panel for the romantic bedroom fireplace and the donkey for the shed/home studio for the Arlington House.
www.francescaspringolo.com

Mary Steingesser:
Mary Steingesser of ArtZMary Studio is the Room Captain in charge of the Arlington home office/artist studio. This room, once a shed, was a huge challenge. Marybrought together a diverse group of artists from SALI and other artist friends to complete a whimsical room decorated with several complicated murals. She even created the ceiling moldings and hand painted the framed flower paintings. Mary has a BA from the University of New Hampshire and is an accomplished artist specializing in fine art-but her passion is abstract art and sculpture. Her works have been displayed in many shows and galleries in the DC area.
www.artzmary.com

Wanda Timmons:
Wanda Timmons, has over 18 years experience in wall finishes and owns Designer Finishes, Inc., an Aqua Finishing Solutions™ Studio in Warrensburg, Il. She has pioneered incredibly realistic and beautiful finishes for countertops, furniture and floors. Wanda's work has been featured in model homes in Chatham and Champaign, IL and in the 2004 Showcase of Homes in Mahomet, IL. Her school of faux finishes is well known for exciting and unique finishes. Her Venetian plaster kitchen countertop in the Arlington Project looks just like granite and the marmarino countertop in the wine cellar fooled even a tile contractor!
www.wandafaux.com

Justin Valez-Hagen:
Justin Valez-Hagen, owner of DC Concrete Technologies has over 10 years of experience in the construction industry. A self-proclaimed "creative entrepreneur," Justin has started several companies and enjoys the opportunity his new company affords him to custom design concrete projects. He is also working towards earning an MBA and Law Degree from George Washington University and has plans to expand the company to several other cities by year end 2006. He and his crew completely transformed the front walk and entrance of the house as well as the kitchen and dining room floors.
www.dcconcretetechnologies.com

Adrienne van Dooren
Adrienne van Dooren, Project Chair and author of the House That Faux Built is an experienced faux finisher, artist and instructor. She has trained under master artisans in both the US and Europe. Her work has been featured in numerous magazines, and she has won several prestigious awards to include the LDI Instructor Award and the 2004 International Artist Exchange's Top Award. Highly sought after by designers, she limits her commissioned work to pursue a passion for teaching, mentoring beginning artists. Artist's coop, and participating in charity projects.
www.cefaux.com
www.fauxhouse.com

Carol van Gerena:

Carol van Gerena of Red Lion Stencils completed a canvas panel for the Chicago Church Project using the Red Lion line of Stencils. The panel is 3 x 4' of a crane in water and surrounded with Beaux-Artes Molding. Carol's stencil line has many elements perfect for murals such as fountains, archways etc, great designs for children's rooms and much more. She also has smaller stencils created just for scrapbooking and smaller projects. Useing these stencils with a bit of hand embellishing and shading results in a work of art.
www.redlionstencils.com

Nicola Vigini

A native Italian, attended the prestigious Liceo Artistico in Rome and the Institute Superieure de Peintre Decorative in Paris, He combines a lifetime of artistic training in Europe and America, and is best known as a master of Trompe L'oeil and Grotesca. His wife Leslie is his business partner and innovative instructor of fine finishes at their studio in San Antonio, TX. Together they host an annual painting trip to Italy with top guest instructors for an unforgettable experience. Nicola recently released a new line of grotesca stencils and furnished stunning grotesca panels to the Arlington and Chicago projects.
www.viginistudios.com

Barth White:

With over 20 years experience in faux finishing, Barth White is best known for his incredible work in casinos in Las Vegas, the faux capitol of the world. Barth invented the Faux Tool and teaches faux finishing and decorative painting at Barth's Faux Studio in Las Vegas and all across the country. His clients include such world renowned casinos as Caesar's Palace, Rio, Bellagio, Venetian, Paris, Aladdin, and the new Wynn hotel in Las Vegas. Barth applied marmarino to the walls and

a glazed faux finish to the ceiling of the Arlington living room. He also fauxed and distressed the dated fireplace, molding and doors.
www.faux.com

Caroline Woldenberg:

Caroline Woldenberg began her career as a interior designer, then found her passion for painting in 1987. Her projects have taken her throughout the United States, as well as to the Marias district of Paris and the fashion district of Milan. Based in Atlanta, her company has been servicing the area's top designers as a full service decorative arts company for residential, large commercial and religious installations. Their services include wall finishes, plastering, murals, painted furnishings, and gilding. Caroline has a reputation as one of the best faux and furniture instructors in the country. Her work has been featured in Southern Accents, Veranda, and House Beautiful. She is the designer and finisher for the Arlington kitchen.
www.thefinishingschoolatl.com

Josh Yavelberg:

At the age of thirteen, Josh Yavelberg began studying the human figure at the University of Miami under the instruction of professor Luis Ulman . He later studied at Pratt Institute for Art and Design in Brooklyn, New York where he obtained a B.S. as well as a Master's Degree in Art History. Josh currently lives in the Washington, D.C. Metro area pursuing his own artwork as well as portrait and mural commissions. While incorporating his knowledge of Art history with his artwork, much of his work has been described as "ambitious" and "impressive." The main goal has been to provide the viewer with an opportunity to interact and connect with his works of art while expressing the world from a unique point of view. Josh painted the woman in towel, basement closet. Arlington
www.yavelbergstudios.com

Rose Wilde

Rose and Jack Wilde founded the Wood Icing Company in 2000. It became Rose's brainchild when she discovered this new way to add dimension and texture to furniture. She quickly discovered that others found her invention to be so intriguing, that she now has a patent pending. The day she invented the Wood Icing technique, she knew she was onto something big. It was unique, versatile, and durable. She made piece after piece, impressing her friends and family and newfound clients. The word spread quickly, and soon she received client referrals and calls from decorators asking for custom pieces. This newfound passion of hers was a hit. Now, she and her husband, Jack, manage The Wood Icing Company full time. The growing demand for the innovative Wood Icing technique and products has prompted the Wildes to make the products available online. Rose accomplished the amazing cabinet makeover in the shed.
www.woodicing.com

David Galen of Galen studios, Leesburg, VA. David specializes in architectural photography and has been published in several other books and magazines. His customers include: Georgetown University, G&M Homes, United Airlines, Red, Hot & Blue, Concrete Masonry Designs Magazines and many other high profile companies.
www.galenphoto.com

100 Hour Volunteers:

Carl Bayer
Ceil Glembloci
Rebecca Hotop
Chris Jackson
Linda ONeill
Carol Patterson
Ashley Spencer
Caroline Spenser
Celeste Stuart
Lisa Turner
Tracie Weir

Volunteers:

Sandi Anderson
Sheri Anderson
Christine Barnette
Khacki Berry
Carolyn Blahosky
Steve Brown
Patricia Buzzo
Heavenly Campbell
Melissa Clements
Ann Cook
Sandra Davis
Debbie Dennis
Ernie Dominguez
Karen Derrico
Mitch Eanes
Carol Farley
Reginal Flemming
Hope Gibbs
Michael Gross
Susan Guarino
Joan Hagan
Andrea Held
Lee Hickman
Susan Huber
Ryoko Kanker
Kathy Karrol
Emily Kato
Kathy Keel
Mark Ketteran
Li Lammert
Elizabeth Lee
Anne Lemarie
John Leonard
Lewis Lewis
Hector Lopez
Jonathon Lutz
Denise Malueg
Linda Manning
Sylvia Martorana
Stacey Matarese
Rosalie Myers
Kate Nagel
Laura Nalley
Dennis Nash
Patrick O'Neill

Phyllis Palmer
David Reyes
Cathi Rinn
Carol Rohrbaugh
Kathleen Sackry
Ian Seabock
Russell Sellineer
Jacky Shaw
Sue Sidun
Pauline Siple
Sally Skene
Jennifer Skene
Donna Smith
Francesca Springolo
Peter Spencer
Piers Spencer
Karen Steele
Marc Steingesser
Rachel Steingesser
Vicki Suazo
Amanda Summerlin
Wanda Swierczynski
Debbie Thompson
Barb Tise
Robert Turner
Jenny Vanier-Walter
Carol Van Gerena
Sharon Van Meter
Eric Whiteside
Chris Woodruff
Belinda Yoder

You dig us... We dig you!

You dig us... We dig you!

Fabrics:

Calico Corners
Wide selection of designer fabrics, supplies and full service fabrication
6400 Williamsburg Blvd.
Arlington, VA 22207
703-536-5488
www.calicocorners.com

Discount Fabrics, USA
Designer fabrics at a fraction of the cost
308 Hillswood Ave.
Falls Church, VA 22046
703-241-1555

Learning Resources:

Art Leagues:
Great resource for meeting other artists and expanding knowledge. Most hold monthly meetings, classes and provide newsletters on upcoming shows, classes and exhibit/ Show opportunities. Most areas have an Art League --just do an on-line search for one in your community . For example in the DC area there is the Reston League of Artists, Springfield Art League and others. The largest is:

The Art League
105 North Union Street
Alexandria, VA 22314
Gallery: 703-683-1780
School: 703-683-2323
www.theartleague.org

Concrete DÈcor Magazine Online, The Journal for Decorative Concrete
Directory of How-To tips, calendar of training seminars and events and decorative concrete training directory.
228 Grimes
Eugene, OR 97402
877-935-8906
Info@protradepub.com
www.concretedecor.net

Fauxcademy of Decorative Finishing
National awards conference for faux and decorative artists. Includes awards and trophies in multiple categories plus great learning opportunities: seminars, roundtable discussions, masterminds and demonstrations.
800-980-3289 toll-free
800-621-3289 fax
www.fauxcademy.com

Faux Effects World Magazine Distributed by Faux Effects
International. Available at Barnes & Noble. Includes Faux and Decorative painting ideas and articles featuring FEI products. (Also check out the Meeting of the Masters Conferences for demonstrations and meeting other faux finishers)
3435 Aviation Blvd.
Vero Beach, FL 32960
800-270-8871
772-778-9653 fax
Editor@fauxeffectsworld.com
www.fauxeffectsworld.com

The Faux Finisher Magazine
Articles about and for Faux Finishers and Decorative Painters.
Distributed by PRDA which also has training and certification classes
403 Axminister Drive
Fenton, MO 63026-2941
636-326-2636
636-326-1823 fax
www.fauxfinishermagazine.com

Faux Forum.com
An online forum for decorative painting professionals to share information
www.fauxforum.com

Murals Plus
On-line discussion groups for faux finishers and muralists, with professional moderators. Includes photo postings and archived help and tips.
www.muralsplus.com

PaintPRO
The Professional Painter s Journal A free digital magazine with information, ideas, calendar of events & training and a directory of painting schools.
228 Grimes
Eugene, OR 97402
877-935-8906
Info@protradepub.com
www.paintpro.net

Professional Decorative Painters Association
2132 Market Street
Denver, CO 80205
303-893-0330
Info@pdpa.org
www.pdpa.org

SALI
Stencil Artisans League, Inc. Includes stencil, faux and decorative painting. Chapters in many local communities, classes and a national painting convention offering mini-classes by the nations top artists.
P.O. Box 3109
Los Lunas, NM 87031
505-865-9119 phone/fax
Salihelp@aol.com
www.sali.org

In DC area: SALI-DC Capital Area Decorative Artisans
Ceil Glembocki, President
911 Saddleback Ct.
McLean, VA 22102-1317
703-790-1984
Virginiaegg@cox.net

Maryland Chapter: Chesapeake Bay Stencilers
Amy Ketteran, President
Mt. Airy, MD
410-772-1221
www.ketteranstudios.com
Amy@ketteranstudios.com

Online Chapter: Stenciling Roundtable (SRT)
Laura Ross
www.stencilingroundtable.org

Paint Decor
Available at local bookstores

Decorating Solutions Magazines
Available at local bookstores

Paint Magic
Available at local bookstores

Recipe Card Learning Series
Bob Marx, Executive Director
50 Carnation Ave, Bldg. #2
Floral Park, NY 11001
516-327-4850/
516-327-4853 fax
finschool@aol.com
www.thefinishingschool.com

Society of Decorative Painters
Have chapters in many local communities holding monthly meetings and classes. Excellent regional and national painting conferences offering mini-classes by the nations top artists393 N. McLean
Wichita, KS 67203
316-269-9300
www.decorativepainters.org

Concrete and Stone:

Gary Arvanitopulos
Shed entrance, modello on kitchen entrance and waterfall fountain
814-838-2281
703-831-1383
Gary@exquisite-finishes.com
Arvanit@velocity.net
www.exquisite-finishes.com

Bella Vernici Architectural Concrete and Stains
(as seen on wine cellar floor)
200 Centre Blvd.
Suite #17
Burleson, TX 76028
888-508-FAUX (3289)
Artist@BellaVernici.com
www.bellavernici.com

Bella Vernici Decorative Concrete Overlay System
Distribution by Paintin the Town Faux
2830 Holcomb Bridge Rd.
Alpharetta, Georgia 30022
770-641-7641
770-641-3094 fax
800-549-0414
www.paintinthetown.com
Info@paintinthetown.com

Coral-Lite
Faux Stone Products Interior/Exterior lightweight faux stone decorative pieces, fireplace surrounds and more. (as seen on master bathtub)
Distributed by Artimatrix
www.artimatrix.com/shop_coral_light.htm

D.C. Concrete Technologies
Decorative Concrete Application in the DC area (front walk and kitchen floor)
Justin Velez-Hagan
1-800-283-9498
202-558-6562 FAX
Justin@dcconcretetechnologies.com
www.dcconcretetechnologies.com

Decorative Concrete of Maryland, Inc.
Specializing in Decorative Overlays & Indoor/Outdoor Water Features (as seen on kitchen countertop and side entrance)
Dan Mahlmann
Olney, MD
301-325-1544
301-774-6034-fax
dcmofmd@verizon.net
www.decorativeconcreteofmd.com

Pure Texture
Cement Products donated for fountain project
517 Medley Street
Greensboro, NC 27406
336-335-3010
336-574-0802 fax
www.puretexture.com

Skimstone
Specialty product toweled over concrete or used with specialty primer over floors walls and countertops
Rudd Company, Inc.
1141 NW 50th St.
Seattle, WA 98107
206-789-1000/206-789-1001 fax
Info@skimstone.com
www.skimstone.com

Twig and a Feather, Inc.
Sculpted Walls /Dimensional and stained concrete overlays in the Chicago area.
  Keren Andra Navarro
  1051 East Main, Suite 102
  East Dundee, Ill 60118
  847-426-2377
  847-426-2366 FAX

Elephants on the Wall
Paint by the number style mural transfers (such as those seen in the Chicago kid s room)
  2535 N. Altadena Drive
  Altadena, CA 91001
  626-794-1415
  www.elephantsonthewall.com

Murals Your Way
An on-line resource for purchasing economical preprinted murals (such as the Tuscan mural in the Arlington wine cellar arch)
  717 5th Street South
  Hopkins, MN 55343
  888-295-9764
  952-938-4808 fax
  www.muralsyourway.com

Hanging Treasures
  hangingtreasurers@yahoo.com

**Alexandria Paint &
Decorative Center**
  3610 E. King St.
  Alexandria, VA 22302
  703-379-5800

**Arlington Paint &
Decorative Center**
  5701 Lee Highway
  Arlington, VA 22207
  703-534-4477

Art-Stuf
Suppliers of art, leaf and molding supplies
  730 Bryant Street
  San Francisco, CA 94107
  1-888-ART-STUF
  www.artstuf.com

Beaux-Artes
Decorative grates, hinge straps, moldings, etc
  1012 South Creek View Ct.
  Churchton, MD 20733
  410-867-0790
  410-867-8004 fax
  www.beaux-artes.com
  Info@beauxartes.com

BEHR Paints
  www.behr.com or call 1-800-854-0133,
  Ext. 2 for more information.
Sold exclusively at The Home Depot.

Benjamin Moore Paints
  51 Chestnut Ridge Road
  Montvale, NJ 07645
  Info@benjaminmoore.com
  www.benjaminmoore.com

Briste Group
paints, plasters and supplies sold at paint stores nation-wide
  905-443-0998
  888-465-5571
  Bristegroup@allstream.net
  www.bristegroup.com

**Color Wheel Paints
& Coatings**
DC area paints, supplies and classes
  Eric Crow
  1374 chain Bridge Rd.
  McLean, VA 22101
  703-356-8477
  www.colorwheel.com

Daige Pro-Cote Waxer
  800 645-3323
  fax: (516) 621-1916
  info@daige.com
  www.daige.com

(All schools teach Faux/ Decorative painting unless alternative specialty is noted Italics)

DecoFinish, LLC
  2012 NE 155th St.
  North Miami Beach, FL 33162
  305-940-8022
  305-940-8411
  www.decofinish.com
  Info@decofinish.com

Faux Design Studio
Chicago s Premier School of Decorative Arts /Faux Effects® International Distributor
  101 N. Swift Rd.
  Addison, IL 60101
  630-627-1011
  630-627-1012 fax
  Fauxdesignstudio@ameritech.net
  www.fauxdesignstudio.com

Faux Fingers
Miniature trowels used for corners, small spaces and VP murals
  1713 Woodwind
  Austin, Texas 78758
  412-963-4767
  www.fauxfingers.com
  Sales@fauxfingers.com

Faux Mart
Discounted faux finishing tools and supplies, wholesale and retail
  2830 Holcomb Bridge Rd.
  Alpharetta Georgia 30022
  770-641-0884
  888-474-0042 toll-free
  770-641-3094 fax
  www.fauxmart.com
  Info@fauxmart.com

Faux Masters Retail Store
Faux Effects® International Distributor
  22941 Savi Ranch Parkway
  Yorba Linda, CA 92887
  888-977-3289
  Info@fauxmasters.com
  www.fauxmasters.com

The Faux Store
Aqua Finishing Solutions™ and Faux Effects® International Professional line available through
  www.fauxstore.com

Golden Artist Colors, Inc.
Artists colors mediums and textural supplies
  188 Bell Road
  New Berlin, NY 13411-9527
  607-847-6154
  800-959-6543
  607-847-9228 fax
  www.goldenpaints.com

Krylon
While the nation s leading spray paint manufacturer, they also have exciting specially, faux, & water based paints.
  101 Prospect Ave., NW
  540 Midland Building
  Cleveland, OH 44115
  1-8004KRYLON (1-800-457-9566)
  www.krylon.com

Luminex USA
U.S distributor of Fiber-optic fabrics
  12212 Technology Blvd
  Austin, TX 78727
  888-219-8020
  512-219-5195 fax
  Info@luminexcorp.com
  www.luminexcorp.com

Modern Masters, Inc.
Best known for their metallic paints
  9380 San Fernando Road
  Sun Valley, CA 91352
  818-683-0201
  800-942-3166
  818-683-0202-FAX
  Info@modernmastersinc.com
  www.modernmasters.com

Oikos
Solvent-free decorative systems/plasters (as seen in the Arlington bath) Avail in paint stores
  www.oikos-paint.com

**Parvati Textures Cotton
Plaster**
Wallcovering System Distribution by Paintin the Town Faux
  2830 Holcomb Bridge Rd.
  Alpharetta, Georgia 30022
  770-641-7641
  770-641-3094 fax
  800-549-0414
  www.parvatitextures..com
  Info@paintinthetown.com

Plaza Artist Materials
Art supplies, DC area
  8209 Georgia Ave.
  Silver Spring, MD 20910
  301-587-5581
  customercare@plazaart.com
  www.plazaart.com

Pro Faux
Faux products, tools and classes
  1367 Girard Street
  Akron, Ohio 44301
  330-773-1983
  www.profaux.com

Roc-Lon
Painting and floor-cloth canvas
  410-522-2545
  www.roc-lon.com
  Dsanders@roc-lon.com

Scentco
Scented paint additives
  93 Genesis Parkway
  Thomasville, GA 31792
  877-723-6826
  229-228-6137 fax
  www.scentco.net
  Info@scentco.net

**The Sherwin-Williams
Company**
Local store sponsored DC project
  Matt Keaney
  10880 Main Street
  Fairfax, VA 22030
  703-591-3770
  www.sherwin-williams.com

Sinopia
Finest quality pigments and materials for restoration, interior design and fine arts.
  3385 Twentysecond Street
  San Francisco, CA 94110
  415-824-3180
  415-824-3280 fax
  Pigments@sinopia.com
  www.sinopia.com

Wing Enterprises
Little Giant Ladders: Multitask ladders that configure for stairs, uneven bases, varied hieghts and mini scaffold.
  www.littlegiantladders.com

The Wood Icing Company
Textural finishing products that transform furniture, etc (as seen in shed cabinet, Arlington)
  P.O. Box 8
  Foristell, MO 63348
  866-966-3423
  636-673-2070 fax
  Rosewilde@woodicing.com
  www.woodicing.com

Zuzka for Fabricology Inc.
  37 East 18th Street, 10th Floor
  New York, New York 10003
  212-260-1876
  212-260-7963 fax
  www.zuzka.com
  Info@zuzka.com

Resources

Anything but Plain
12539 Duncan Suite D
Houston, TX 77066
281-444-2070
800-444-1170
281-444-2081 fax
Abp@flash.net
www.anythingbutplain.com

Artimatrix Academy of Architectural Finishes
230 N. Mosley Suite A.
Old Town Wichita, KS 67202
316-264-2789
Info@artimatrix.com
www.artimatrix.com

Barth's Faux Studio
Barth White, Director
3520 Coleman St.
North Las Vegas, NV 89032
702-631-5959
800-998-3289
www.faux.com

Buon Frescos Academy of Wall Artistry
Victoria J. Bingham, Director
Offering world class instruction
by award winning instructors of
fine surface finishing
Metro Washington DC
703-914-5606 local
888-637-3726 toll-free
AWA@bfresco.com
www.bfresco.com

Chicago Institute of Fine Finishes
Kathy Carroll, President
504 East St. Charles Rd.
Carol Stream, IL 60188
800-797-4305
630-653-2400
630-653-4671 fax
Kcarroll@fauxbykathy.com
www.fauxbykathy.com

Classical Art Studios
800-766-8712
www.fauxtastic.com
Randying@optionline.net

Color Alchemist School & Restorations
John Leanard
202-679-5525
P.O. Box 50362
Arlington, VA 22205
Johnleanard@cox.com

Creative Enterprises
Artist Coop. and Referral
Network. Adrienne also guest
teaches at studios worldwide
Adrienne van Dooren
7317 Castleberg Court
Alexandria, VA
703-971-8252
Info@cefaux.com
www.cefaux.com

Crosby-Amblard Studios
Murals and figures
Sean Crosby and
Pascal Amblard
168 Elkton Road, Suite 209
Newark, DE 19711
302-731-7752
Crosby-amblard-studio@comcast.net
www.crosby-amblard-studios.com

Designer Finishes
Wanda Timmons, Director
266 North State Route 121
Warrensburg, IL 62573
217-672-8822
217-672-3737 fax
www.wandafaux.com
Wandat@wandafaux.com

Donna's Designs Faux Finish & Business Workshop
Donna Mabrey, Director
Atlanta, GA
770-985-2285 (Local)
1-877-884-7935 (Toll-free)
www.learnfaux.com
donna@learnfaux.com

The Faux Finish School
Martin Alan Hirsch Decorative
Finishes Studio
Louisville, KY
800-598-FAUX
www.fauxfinish.com

Faux Happenings Institute
Anna Torre-Smith, Director
301-279-2222
301-279-0843 fax
Info@fauxhappenings.com
www.fauxhappenings.com

Faux Design Studio
Sheri Zeman & Jacek
Prowinski
101 N. Swift Rd.
Addison, IL 60101
630-627-1011
630-627-1012 fax
www.fauxdesignstudio.com
Fauxdesignstudio@ameritech.net

Faux Effects® International Fine Finishing Studio
3435 Aviation Blvd. Suite A
Vero Beach, FL 32960
772-778-9044
800-270-8871
772-778-9653 fax
Studio@fauxfx.com
www.fauxeffects.com

Faux Like a Pro
Mark London
119 Braintree Street
Allston, MA 02134
888-765-4950
617-254-8898
617-254-8899 fax
www.fauxlikeapro.com

Kelly King Institute of Decorative Finishes
Faux plus furniture finishing.
The Faux Finish Institute by
Kelly S. King is one of the
nation's foremost instructional
schools in the art of decorative
wall and furniture finishes.
14851 West Highway 6
Gretna, NE 68028
800-980-3289 - toll free
800-621-3289 - fax
Info@fauxfinishinstitute.com
www.fauxfinishinstitute.com

Faux Masters Studio
The Hoppe Brothers
22855-E Savi Ranch Parkway
Yorba Linda, Ca 92887
888-977-3289
Info@fauxmasters.com
www.fauxmasters.com

The Faux School Maryland
Ron Layman, Director
5711 Industry Lane, Suite 28
Frederick, MD 21704

The Faux School Florida
663 Harold Ave.
Winter park, FL 32789
1-877-GET-FAUX
301-668-5100
301-228-3100 fax
Sales@thefauxschool.com
www.thefauxschool.com

Faux Works
Barbara Skivington, Director
2638 Willard Dairy Road
Suite 106
High Point, NC 27265
336-841-0130
Info@fauxworksstudio.com
www.fauxworksstudio.com

FE Dallas, Inc.
4550 Sunbelt Dr.
Addison, TX 75001
972-733-0028
Info@fedallas.com
www.fedallas.com

The Finishing School New York
Bob Marx, Executive Director
50 Carnation Ave, Bldg. #2
Floral Park, NY 11001
516-327-4850/
516-327-4853 fax
finschool@aol.com
www.thefinishingschool.com

The Finishing School - Pennsylvania
Carol Kemery, Studio Director
507 North York St.
Mechanicsburg, PA 17055
717-790-3190
717-790-3191 fax
Finschoolpa@aol.com
www.thefinishingschool.com

The Finishing School - Atlanta
Caroline Woldenberg, Studio
Director
2086 Faulkner Rd.
Atlanta, GA 30324
404-929-9522
404-929-9523 fax
Admin@thefinishingschoolatl.com
www.thefinishingschoolatl.com

School of Italian Plasters Decoration Academy - Georgia
James and Shayna Kirkpatrick
1717 Spring Street
Smyrna, GA 30080
866-560-4444 Toll Free
770-438-0870 Direct Line
770-438-7709 Fax
www.italianplasters.com
James@italianplasters.com
Doyle@italianplasters.com

-San Diego
Doyle and Linda Self
2145b Fern Street
San Diego, CA 92104
619-282-0120

Jennifer Rebecca Designs
Studio of Decorative Finishes
Jennifer Huehns &
Rebecca Klein
Minneapolis/St. Paul, MN
763-792-9244
Studio@jenniferrebeccadesigns.com
www.jenniferrebeccadesigns.com

Karibeth Creations, Inc.
Decorative Painting Studio
17681 Kenwood Trail
Lakeville, MN 55044
952-898-9155
www.karinbethcreations.com

Ketteran Studios
Mt. Airy, MD
410-772-1221
www.ketteranstudios.com
Amy@ketteranstudios.com

Liliedahl Fine Art Studio
Liliedahl Video Productions
Classical Oil Painting
Johnnie Liliedahl
808 South Broadway St.
La Porte, TX 77571-5324
877-867-0324 Toll Free
281-867-0324
www.johnnieliliedahl.com
www.lilipubs.com

The Mad Stencilist
Airbrush, stenciling, murals
P.O. Box 219
Diamond Springs, CA 95619
888-882-6232 - toll-free
530-626-8618 - fax
www.madstencilist.com
Questions@madstencilist.com

Paintin the Town, Faux
Susie Goldenberg, Director
2830 Holcomb Bridge Rd.
Alpharetta, Georgia 30022
770-641-7641 P
770-641-3094 F
1-800-549-0414
www.paintinthetown.com
email- info@paintinthetown.com

Distributor: Aqua finishing
Solutions, Bella Vernici, Parvati,
etc and 5000 sq ft training
facility

Patina Studios
1620 W. 39th Street
Kansas City, MO 64111
816-561-4103
Learn@patinastudios.com
www.patinastudios.com

Pierre Finkelstein Institute of Decorative Painting, Inc.
20 West 20th Street, Suite
1009
New York, NY 10011
888 FAUX ART
212-352-2058 fax
Pfinkel@earthlink.net
www.pfinkelstein.com

Priscilla Hauser Decorative Painting Seminars by the Sea

P.O. Box 521013
Tulsa, OK 74152-1013
918-743-6072
918-743-5075 fax
PHauser376@aol.com
www.priscillahauser.com

Prismatic Painting Studios

Gary Lord
11126 Deerfield PRd.
Cincinnati, OH 45242
513-931-5520
513-931-5545 fax
Info@prismaticpainting.com
www.prismaticpainting.com

Pro Faux Workshops

1367 Girard Street
Akron, Ohio 44301
330-773-1983
www.profaux.com

Sarasota School of Decorative Arts

5376 Catalyst Ave.
Sarasota, FL 34233
888-454-3289 toll free
941-921-6181
941-921-9494 fax
Info@ssda1.com
www.ssda1.com

Stencilwerks School of Decorative Painting

1918 Tilghman Street
Allentown, PA 18104
800-357-4954
610-289-7792 fax
www.stencilwerks.com
Stencilwerks@rcn.com

Twig and a Feather, Inc.

Concrete and Sculpted Walls
Keren Andra Navarro
President/Owner
1051 East Main
Suite 102
East Dundee, Ill 60118
847-426-2377
847-426-2366 FAX
Admin@twigandafeather.com

Tust Studio

P.O. Box 2245
Pine, AZ 85544
928-476-3344
866-728-1107 fax
www.tuststudio.com
Email laura@tuststudio.com

The Wood Icing Company

P.O. Box 8
Foristell, MO 63348
866-966-3423
636-673-2070 fax
Rosewilde@woodicing.com
www.woodicing.com

Vigini Studios

Also has summer Italian
Workshop
2531 Boardwalk
San Antonio, TX 78217
210-212-6177
210-212-6183 fax
Info@viginistudios.com
www.viginistudios.com

Services:

Catering:
Anne-Marie Schmidt

Star Cattering
2000 Mt Vernan Ave
Alexandria, VA 22310
(703) 549-8090
www.starcateringevents.com

Keep My Pet
Pet preservation

Preserves your choices and your
pet. Special process for pets
(not taxidermy)
Service across the USA
www.kepmypet.com
(571) 239-6656

Landscaping by Chris Jackson

Landscape design, service,
stonework, ponds, waterfalls etc
(703) emailed for phone #
Info@rcjacksonlandscaping.com
www.rcjacksonlandscaping.com

Real Estate:
Suzanne Leedy, CRS

McEnearney Associates
suzanne@suzanneleedy.com
www.suzanneleedy.com
(703) 627-5302
fax (703) 528-1556

Remodeling/Custom Homes:
Action Home Construction, Inc.

Joe Meager
4909 Lincoln Ave
Alexandra, VA 22312
(703) 914-5655

Valerie Burchett

Website design
5436 Butterfield Drive
Colorado Springs, CO 80918
Burchett@gmail.com

York Graphic Services

Printing, finishing, mailing and
fulfillment, website and CD
development
3650 W. Market St.
York, PA 17404
717-505-9701
www.ygsc.com
Info@ygsc.com

Stencils:

Andreae Designs

P.O. Box 300160
Waterford, MI 48330
888-826-3403
www.mystencils.com
Andreaedesigns@hotmail.com

Buckingham Stencils

1710 Morello Road
Nanoose Bay B.C. Canada
V9P 9B1
888-468-9221
866-468-9227 fax
www.buckinghamstencils.com

Jan Dressler Stencils

Mylar and adhesive stencils
253 SW 41st Street
Renton, WA 98055-4930
888-656-4515 toll-free
425-656-4515 local
425-656-4381 fax
www.dresslerstencils.com
customerservice@dresslerstencils.com

Heart of the Home Stencils

17516 Chesterfield
Airport Road, Cabin B
Chesterfield, MO
636-519-1768
888-675-1695 toll free
208-279-2570
www.stencils4u.com

Lynn Brehm Designs

6827 Caminito Sueno
Carlsbad, CA 92009
760-744-3986
LSBDesigns@aol.com
www.natural-accents.com

The Mad Stencilist

P.O. Box 219 Dept. N
Diamond Springs, CA 95619
888-882-6232 - toll-free
530-626-8618 - fax
www.madstencilist.com
Questions@madstencilist.com

Modello™ Designs

Adhesive stencils and specialty
floor and ceiling pattern sets
2504 Transportation Ave.,
Suite H
National City, CA 91950
800-663-3860
800-747-9767
619-477-5607/619-477-0373
fax
Sales@modellodesigns.com
www.modellodesigns.com

Red Lion Stencils

1232 First NH Tpk
Northwood, NH 03261
603-942-8949
603-942-8769 fax
www.redlionstencils.com
Lion@redlionstencils.com

Royal Design Studio

2504 Transportation Ave.
Suite H
National City, CA 91950
619-477-3559
800-747-9767
619-477-8193 - fax
Sales@RoyalDesignStudio.com
www.royaldesignstudio.com

SayWhat?

Mylar and SayWhat? adhesive
lettering stencils, Daige waxer
The Mad Stencilist
Attn: SayWhat?
P.O. Box 219
Diamond Springs, CA 95619
888-882-6232 - toll free
530-626-8618 - fax
SayWhat@madstencilist.com
www.madstencilist.com/saywhat/
lettering.htm

Stencil Kingdom

28 Greville Road
Kenilworth, Warwickshire,
CV8 1EL
+44(0) 19260513050
Julie@stencilkingdom.com
www.stencilkingdom.com

Stencil Planet

P.O. Box 90
Berkeley Heights, NJ 07922
877-836-2457 toll free
908-771-8910 fax
Info@stencilplanet.com
www.stencilplanet.com

Stencilwerks

1918 Tilghman St.
Allentown, PA 18104
800-357-4954
610-289-7792 fax
www.stencilwerks.com
Stencilwerks@rcn.com

Vigini Studios

Line of grottesca stencils
2531 Boardwalk
San Antonio, TX 78217
210-212-6177
210-212-6183 fax
Info@viginistudios.com
www.viginistudios.com
663-3860
619-477-5607
619-477-0373 fax
Sales@modellodesigns.com
www.modellodesigns.com

A sincere thank you to all our sponsors. Without you there would be no "House that Faux Built"
Special thanks to our platinum sponsors bolded below for your generous support.

PLATINUM SPONSORS:
Andreae Designs
Artimatrix
Ashley Spencer
Barth's Faux Studio
Beaux-Artes Faux and Moldings
BG Decorative Paint
Crosby-Amblard-studios
Creative Enterprises
Designer Finishes
Fauxcademy
Faux and Fleur
Faux Design Studio
Faux Effects®, International
The Finishing Source, Atlanta
Gary Lord Wall Options
Jmiles Studios
Ketteran Studios
Kelly King, The Institute of Fine Finishes
The Mad Stencilist
Mary Stengesser
Modello Designs
O'Neill Studios
Nancy and Walt Petrie
Paintin the Town Faux
RMR Associates
Royal Design Studio
Sarasota School of Decorative Arts, Inc.
Seabock Studios
Suzanne Leedy-McEnearney Associates
Taperan Studio
Thompson Creek Windows
Vigini Studios

GOLD:
Chris Jackson Landscaping
Keep My Pet
Kingslan & Gibilisco Decorative Arts
Pierre Finkelstein Inst. of Dec. Painting, Inc.
Leonard Pardon
Roc-Lon
The Wood Icing Company
Omar Salinas –hightec photography

SILVER:
Classical Art Studios
Michel Nadai
Patricias-Palette /Patricia Buzzo and Andreas

BRONZE:
Exsitement Graphics
Arlington Paint & Decorating Center
Art Stuf
Behr Paints
Calico Corners
Color Wheel Paints and Coatings:
  • Adicolor
  • Benjamin Moore
  • Briste Group
  • Modern Masters
  • Oikos
  • Skimstone
CoralLite
DC Concrete Technologies
Decorative Concrete of Maryland, Inc
Dominion Floors
Elephants on the Wall
Faux by Kathy
Faux like a Pro
Golden Artist Colors, Inc.

Hanging Treasures
Krylon Paints
Liliandahl Studios
Noland Plumbing Supplies
Oriental Rugs and More
PROFAUX
School of Italian Plasters
Star Catering
Wing Enterprises
York Graphic Services
Yves Art

GENERAL:
Action Iron,LLC
art by o'neill
Bella Vernici Studios
Bray and Scarff, Lee Hwy
Brown Construction
Buckingham Stencils
Buon Fresco
Calvert's Fountains and ponds
Ceil Glemblocki
Color Alchemist School & Restoration
Decofinish
Discount Fabrics USA
Donna's Designs
Exquisite-Finishes
Faux Fingers
Faux Mart
Faux Products
Gallen Photography
Globe Bath & Kitchen Remodeling
Hatchers Floors
Heart of the Home Stencils
Jan Dresler Stencils
Julie Kriss, McEnearney Associates, Inc
Kim Wadford

Karabeth Creations
Rebecca Hotop.
Sherwin-Williams Company, Fairfax, VA
Parvati Textures.com
Priscilla Hauser
Hope Gibbs
Jan Dressler Designs
Jennifer-Rebecca Designs
Tim and Marie Tibor
mural guys
Mirror guy
Laser Excel
Luminex USA
Lynn Brehm Stencils
Murals Your Way
McEnearney Associates general
Patina studios ltd
Pure Texture
Plaza Artists Materials and
Picture Framing
PROFAUX
Red Lion Stencils
Roma
Scentco
Schmitt, Dorothy, Landscape Design
School of Italian Plasters
Sherwin Williams International
Sinopia
Stencil Kingdom
Stencil Planet
Stencilwerks
Storehouse® Furniture
Susie-Darrell-Smith
Tim Poe-Antique Mirror Patina Solution
Tust Studio
Twig and a Feather, Inc.
Wall Transformation Designs
Westover Florist
ZB Kids Designs

THE HOUSE THAT FAUX BUILT

Transform Your Home From Shabby to Showplace Using Paints, Plasters & Creativity

Name _____

Address _____

City, State, Zip _____

Phone # _____

Email Address _____

Book - Quantity _____ @ $39.95 each $ _____

Shipping and Handling _____ @ 3.95 each $ _____

Maryland Residents add 5% sales tax ($2.00 each) $ _____

TOTAL $ _____

Discount available for large orders:
Orders of 20 - 49, include 35% discount plus shipping
Orders over 50, include 40% discount plus shipping

All prices subject to change.

Check Attached # _____ Mastercard _____ Visa _____

Card # _____ Exp _____ / _____

Signature _____

MAIL TO: Patti Irwin
The House That Faux Built
3800 Colony Point Place
Edgewater, MD 21037

EMAIL: sales@fauxhouse.com